People Management Skills in Practice

This practical text covers the essential aspects of managing employees, providing relevant and interesting case studies to enable students to develop the management skills and approaches needed at all levels. The book includes a wealth of case studies across industries including public relations, gaming, food service, healthcare, and nonprofits, and hailing from several regions and cultures (including Australia, the Philippines, US, and Taiwan).

The five core sections of the text each focus on a specific managerial skillset: dilemmas managers face when creating a positive work culture, power and influencing others, conflict within a team, managing a cross-cultural team, and motivating and fostering employee engagement. Within each section, short case studies feature real-life situations and managers who had to assess and respond to various challenges with subordinates, colleagues, or their immediate boss. Each case is supported by a case synopsis, reflective questions, and related learning activities. Instructors have access to teaching notes for each case that provide detailed discussion questions, an overview of concepts and their academic references, advanced reading suggestions, and activities that can be employed in class or as supplemental learning assignments.

Comprehensive and practical, this case textbook is the perfect core reading for any postgraduate managerial skills course, MBA, professional qualifications in management and leadership, and degree apprenticeship programs.

Laurie L. Levesque is an associate professor of management at Suffolk University where she co-leads a community of practice around case writing and teaching. Her publications appear in *The Case Journal*, *The Case Research Journal*, the *International Journal of Instructional Cases*, *Academy of Management Review*, *Organization Science*, *Journal of Management Education*, *Management Teaching Review*, and as the featured case in the *Case Writing Workbook*, 3rd edition. She earned a doctorate from Carnegie Mellon University.

International Cases in Business and Management

Series Editors: Gina Vega and Rob Edwards

This series of textbooks has been developed to provide students and lecturers with high-quality, peer-reviewed and concise teaching cases, which explore key business and management topics set in real-life scenarios around the world.

All cases included in each book are short - between 1500 and 2500 words - and are crafted to encourage class discussion and critical reflection. Cases are accompanied by a rich range of online resources for instructors, making effective and rewarding discussion in the classroom and corporate training room easy. All cases are real-world, with no composites and no invented situations. Some of them come from secondary sources, some from personal experience, and some from field research.

The series is suitable for all levels of university education, including MBA and Executive Education, and organizational training environments

Doing Business in South Asia
G. V. Muralidhara

Tourism and Hospitality Management in Practice: A Case Study Collection
Rebecca Wilson-Mah

People Management Skills in Practice
A Case Study Collection
Edited by Laurie L. Levesque

People Management Skills in Practice

A Case Study Collection

Edited by
Laurie L. Levesque

Routledge
Taylor & Francis Group

LONDON AND NEW YORK

First published 2025
by Routledge
4 Park Square, Milton Park, Abingdon, Oxon OX14 4RN

and by Routledge
605 Third Avenue, New York, NY 10158

Routledge is an imprint of the Taylor & Francis Group, an informa business

© 2025 selection and editorial matter, Laurie L. Levesque; individual chapters, the contributors

Access the Instructor Resources: www.Routledge.com/9781032353074

British Library Cataloguing in Publication Data
A catalogue record for this book is available from the British Library

ISBN: 978-1-032-35308-1 (hbk)
ISBN: 978-1-032-35307-4 (pbk)
ISBN: 978-1-003-32629-8 (ebk)

DOI: 10.4324/9781003326298

Typeset in Optima
by Taylor & Francis Books

Contents

Illustrations

Figures

Tables

Acknowledgements

Without the initiative of Gina Vega and Rob Edwards, editors of the *International Cases in Business Management* series with Taylor and Francis Group, publishing this volume would not have been conceptualized and brought forth. Their previous launch of, and editorial partnership overseeing, the International Journal of Instructional Cases led to us discussing case collections that students and faculty would find useful. As a result, this particular volume was envisioned. It brings together contributions from 21 authors who understand the importance of leaders and managers developing an array of people management skills. Thank you to the contributors: Amanda Patel, Ankur Nandedkar, Apryl Roach, Elizabeth McCrea, Eugene Kutcher, George Kokoros, Gina Vega, Holly Chiu, Joy Jones, Keith Hunter, Kevin Hansen, Lindsey Creapeau, Matheus Fonseca, Monika Hudson, Quinn Cunningham, Ralf Mehnert-Meland, Rifat Mahmud, Rob Edwards, Roger Brown, and Roland Kushner. Grateful appreciation is given to MaryLee Horosewski for her skillful copyediting.

Dean Amy Zeng at Suffolk University encouraged and supported the research and writing of business case studies and the Sawyer Business School faculty embraced the efforts of Jane Zhu, Erin Sullivan, and myself to foster a community of practice around it. We believe cases connect students to businesses and to the various challenges their leaders and employees face in the workplace. It has been a pleasure working with colleagues Regina O'Neill, Nicole O'Brien, Sarah Mellen, George Kokoros, Aimee Williamson, Liane Czirjak, Mike Dunlap, Brenda Bond, Lauren Hajjar, and others who have joined us in these efforts. Our case writing skills have benefitted from working with each other, and by presenting at the annual meetings of The CASE Association and NACRA. Reviewers' feedback is necessary to the writing and revising processes. The information, workshops, and distribution of cases provided by The Case Centre have been essential in all phases of our efforts and we appreciate their personalized approach to supporting schools and case writers.

On a more personal note, I'd like to acknowledge my husband Thom Keith with love and gratitude. He offered unwavering support during this period of intense editing and writing, as well as a sounding board, sanity checks, and a great deal of humor.

Laurie L. Levesque

Contributors

Laurie L. Levesque, Ph.D. is an Associate Professor of Management at Suffolk University where she co-leads a community of practice around case writing and teaching. Her publications appear in *The Case Journal, The Case Research Journal, The International Journal of Instructional Cases, Academy of Management Review, Organization Science, Journal of Management Education,* and *Management Teaching Review,* and as the featured case in the *Case Writing Workbook,* 3rd edition. She earned a doctorate from Carnegie Mellon University.

Roger S. Brown, Ph.D. is an Associate Professor at Northwestern Oklahoma State University, US. Dr. Brown enjoys using experiential techniques in the classroom and uses case analysis in both traditional and online courses. Many of his traditional classes involve using Zoom or Interactive Television to stream to students at other locations.

Holly Chiu, Ph.D. is an Associate Professor at Brooklyn College of City University of New York, USA. Her research interests are knowledge sharing, influence tactics, innovation implementation, and employee motivations. Her works can be found in journals such as *British Journal of Management, Group & Organization Management,* and *Journal of Knowledge Management.*

Lindsey J. G. Creapeau, Ed.D., LALD, CDP is an Assistant Professor at the University of Wisconsin–Eau Claire, USA. She is a Licensed Assisted Living Director, a Certified Dementia Practitioner, and a Fellow of the American College of Health Care Administrators. Her research interests include care for those living with dementia, supporting emerging leaders in the long-term care, and various aspects of the long-term care profession.

Quinn W. Cunningham, Ph.D. is an Associate Professor of Management in the Norm Brodsky College of Business at Rider University, US. She is currently a member of the Board for the Interdisciplinary Network for Group Researchers (INGRoup). Her research interests include team information sharing and psychological safety, and management pedagogy. She has previously published articles in the *Journal of Business and Psychology* and *Organization Management Journal.*

Rob Edwards is CEO of the Neurodiversity & Entrepreneurship Association, UK. He has been an Associate Lecturer at the University of Huddersfield and has an MBA from the University of Bradford. He is Co-Editor of the *International Cases in Business and Management* series (Routledge).

Matheus Fonseca is a business professional based in the US. He holds a BSBA in Management from Suffolk University. Currently serving as the CEO of Moonsworth, Matheus is known for his strategic leadership and innovative approaches in the gaming industry, driving growth and fostering success in his many projects

Kevin Hansen, Ph.D., J.D. LL.M., FACHCA was Chair and Associate Professor for Health Care Administration and Public Health at Bellarmine University and had previously taught and researched at the University of Wisconsin–Eau Claire. As a leader both on- and off-campus, he advocated for elder care rights and worked to improve their quality of life and the care and services they received.

Monika L. Hudson, Ed.D., DBA is a tenured Associate Professor at the University of San Francisco's School of Management and teaches entrepreneurship, family business, organizational behavior and public administration on both the graduate and undergraduate levels. She directs USF's Gellert Family Business Center, which promotes and supports family firms in the San Francisco Bay Area. Her research interests include entrepreneurship, identity and behavior and the strategic implementation of the same within the private, public and nonprofit sectors. In 2022, she was named a Fellow of the Family Firm Institute.

Keith O. Hunter, Ph.D. is a tenured Associate Professor at the University of San Francisco's School of Management. Dr. Hunter instructs undergraduate and graduate students across multiple programs, delivering courses that explore human behavior within organizational and community-based. His research, teaching, and service intersect at the examination and improvement of processes that affect human performance and well-being, often emphasizing the impact of informal social structures and how people perceive each other.

Joy A. Jones, Ph.D. is an Associate Professor at Stockton University. She researches and publishes on leadership communication and has been a keynote speaker and trainer on this topic at numerous conferences, leadership forums, corporations, and non-profit organizations throughout the US. Prior to joining higher education, Dr. Jones worked in media management and production for ESPN and Atlantic Video and served as the Communication Director for the Lt. Governor of Kentucky.

George C. Kokoros, MBA is an Adjunct Professor at Suffolk University, Boston, US. He teaches courses in the Management and Entrepreneurship department focused on leadership and business analysis. George has been a senior leader in many startup and high-growth companies over his career, including Staples and Fortune Brands. He is a Lean Six Sigma green belt and certified Business Advisor.

Roland J. Kushner, Ph.D. is a Professor of Business at Muhlenberg College in Allentown, PA. He holds a BA from Carleton University (Canada) and earned his MBA and PhD from Lehigh University in Bethlehem, PA. He researches strategic management and organizational performance challenges in nonprofit organizations, and the economics of cultural industries.

Eugene J. Kutcher, Ph.D. is an Associate Professor of Management and the Dean of the Norm Brodsky College of Business at Rider University, US. He is currently on the board of the Mid-Atlantic Association of Colleges of Business Administration. His research interests include selection systems and employee engagement. He has published articles in journals including *Performance Improvement Quarterly* and *International Journal of Selection and Assessment*.

Rifat Mahmud, MBA is a Higher Education Professional who presently instructs in secondary education through Kelly Education Services within the Camden County School District, US. He holds a bachelor's degree in Business Administration & Management and a Master of Business Administration from Stockton University, Galloway, NJ. He aspires to pursue an EdD to enhance his expertise and contribute further to the higher education Industry.

Elizabeth A. McCrea, Ph.D. is an Associate Professor at Seton Hall University, US. Her cases have been published in *Entrepreneurship Theory and Practice, Journal of Business Ethics Education*, and the *Case Research Journal*. She is a Fellow and Past President of the Eastern Academy of Management and a member of The CASE Association.

Ralf Mehnert-Meland, J.D. is an Associate Professor at Minnesota State University Moorhead, US. He teaches in the areas of business law, international business, finance, and entrepreneurship. Ralf has published college-level course materials for business law and personal finance. He holds a Juris Doctor from George Washington University, a Bachelor of Arts in Marketing and International Business from Carthage College, and a degree as "Bankkaufmann" in his native Germany.

Ankur Nandedkar, Ph.D. is an Associate Professor at Millersville University of Pennsylvania, US. Dr. Nandedkar is inclined towards pedagogical innovations in online and traditional courses and has led several workshops on active learning in regional, national, and international conferences. He also holds a certificate in online teaching and enjoys integrating technology in his courses.

Amanda S. Patel, Ph.D. is an Assistant Professor at Suffolk University, US. She teaches in the areas of organizational behavior and human resource management. She emphasizes hands-on learning. Her research focuses on employee health and wellbeing. She has published in the *Journal of Applied Psychology* and the *Journal of Management*.

Apryl L. Roach, DBA is a Chief Human Resources Officer (CHRO) with practitioner service in Private, Non-Profit and Local Public Government. She is an Adjunct Professor of Management at Rider University, US and The College of New Jersey, US. She is currently a member of the Doctor of Business Administration (DBA) Advisory Board for Thomas Edison State University, and a member of the Master of Business Administration (MBA) graduate studies Advisory Board for The College of New Jersey. Her research interests include changes in roles and responsibilities relative to human resources (HR) professionals as a result of the Covid-19 pandemic, and strategic business best practices with regards to HR management pedagogy.

Gina Vega, Ph.D. is retired Professor of Corporate Social Responsibility and Entrepreneurship and has had Fulbright assignments in Russia, the UK, and Peru. She is widely published in academic journals. Currently, she is Co-Editor of the *International Cases in Business and Management* series (Routledge).

Introduction

Welcome to the International Cases in Business Management series and this special volume of *People Management Skills in Practice: A Case Study Collection*.

In workplaces managers face interpersonal situations with their subordinates, colleagues, and supervisors that demand an array of people management skills. Developing those skills takes time and a great deal of reflection, but can be expedited through training. This volume is intended to aid in that effort. The 16 cases cover a variety of real situations in which managers had to assess and respond to various challenges.

The recommended **discussions** and **learning activities** associated with these cases have been crafted to build fundamental knowledge and accompanying skills essential in leadership roles of all types. The cases in this volume feature skills relevant to learners who are in, or anticipate being in, front-line or mid-level managerial positions, or senior level executive positions, or who own the company. The compact case format helps learners focus on specific skills. The questions provided develop their analytical thinking using real scenarios and opportunities to apply their course content. The use of shorter cases requires less preparation time without diminishing the opportunity for rich discussion.

Educators and learners new to using cases will also find a **helpful guide** on "Case Preparation and Analysis for Students" following this Introduction. This supplemental resource has been developed by Gina Vega and Rob Edwards, editors of the International Cases in Business Management series.

The **organizations** in these cases vary in their industries (public relations, gaming, food service, healthcare), locations (US, Australia, Philippines, Taiwan), type (for-profit, nonprofit), size and age of the organizations (startups, established firms), and the extent of the focal manager's prior experience (young and inexperienced at managing others, experienced but new to a specific context).

The **topics covered** in this volume are found in management training courses and programs, and undergraduate or graduate courses related to leading, managing, or facilitating employees or workplace teams. The volume is divided into five parts, each with three to four standalone cases related to a theme. Part I deals with dilemmas managers face when attempting to create a positive climate and culture. Part II examines power, including the manager's skills of influencing and working through others. Part III includes cases with conflict within a manager's team or conflict that directly involves the manager. The cases in Part IV explore various struggles managers have when dealing with employees from different cultures. Lastly, Part V deals with issues around motivating subordinates and fostering engagement.

DOI: 10.4324/9781003326298-1

Instructors can request the accompanying Teaching Note for each case by going to www.routledge.com/9781032353074. Once validated as an educator, the Teaching Notes will be available.

While each case is positioned within one section based on the themes, many do in fact present situations that are relevant to other themes within the book. Instructors are encouraged to explore all the teaching notes as they match the cases to the content within their courses or training programs.

Cases by Part: An Overview

The cases are organized around five themes that are discussed in more detail below.

Part I: Creating a Positive Climate and Organizational Culture

The four cases in Part I introduce managerial challenges around creating an inclusive workplace climate that encourages employee engagement. Case 1, "Quiet Springs: Engaging Your Team as a New Leader," follows a manager who joined an existing team and realized that several positive benefits could result if she gained her employees' trust and got them to share their job knowledge with her and each other. Case 2, "Building a (New) Company Culture at Ma Reilly's Café," similarly deals with a new manager, who was also the new owner of the café. Her vision necessitated the creation of trust and rebuilding the company culture from the ground up. Case 3, "Reveal a Mistake to the Boss? Trust and Psychological Safety in a Market Research Team," provides an example of a psychologically safe climate in which employees trusted their manager enough to admit to a potentially costly mistake. In contrast, Case 4, "The Outspoken Contractor: Inclusion and Conflict Across Organizational Boundaries," presents the situation of a company that relied on third-party contractors who were treated as second-class outsiders.

Part II: Navigating Power Relationships

Part II offers three cases that explore the power dynamics between managers and others in the organization. In Case 5, "Employee Voice at Bitfrost: Different Perspectives of Managers and Employees to Voice Behavior," a young company co-founder used power in a way that jeopardized an inclusive climate as well as his employees' voice. In Case 6, "The Undermined Manager: Diversity, Influence Tactics, or Inexperience?," a young manager was challenged by an older subordinate who did not comply with her requests. The case sits at the intersection of age, gender, and cultural norms around a leader's influence. In Case 7, "The Chairman's Jokes: Dealing with a Leader's Inappropriate Behavior," the dynamic was reversed and a leader tried to curtail the offensive and discriminatory behaviors his own boss engaged in with others in the organization.

Part III: Handling Workplace Conflict

The cases in Part III allow learners opportunities to consider and analyze different types of conflict, and then envision possible approaches to managing the situations effectively. In Case 8, "Place of Hope and the Board Meeting Disruption," unexpected conflict centered around one individual erupted at a meeting. After the leader addressed the immediate situation, he considered next steps for a long-term solution as well as reflected on the efficacy of his conflict management in the moment. The situation in Case 9, "Conflict Unveiled: Intergroup Blame between Information Technology Teams," revolved around two departments at odds with one another. Lastly, Case 10, "Bias or Poor Training? The Wine Train Incident," explores conflict that may have arisen from biased employee behavior. It challenges readers to consider what the employee could have done differently and how management could have taken steps post hoc to understand the causes and potential actions to prevent such situations.

Part IV: Managing Cross-Cultural Challenges

The three cases in Part IV bring attention to the difficulties inherent in managing and working with people across cultures. In Case 11, "Culture Clash and the Unraveling of an Immigrant Entrepreneur's American Dream," a frustrated franchisee encountered communication and employee motivation issues. Case 12, "Trust and Communication across Borders: Leadership Challenges at Ellume Health," follows a business owner who dealt with communication and coordination challenges when managing two virtual teams of leaders operating in different countries. Lastly, in Case 13, "When in Rome (or Manila …): Where Business, Law, and Ethics Meet," we learn about an executive who was challenged to behave in ways aligned with his personal values when colleagues put him in an uncomfortable situation while in an unfamiliar cultural context. Together these three cases bring attention to some of the many skills and approaches managers need to handle various cross-cultural challenges they may face in their workplace.

Part V: Motivating Subordinates and Fostering Engagement

The final section of this volume features cases that deal with motivation related to work contribution, incentives, and the retention of workers. In Case 14, "Employee Retention in a PR Firm: Generational Differences or Insufficient Incentives," a business owner tried to incentive employees to stay longer in entry level positions in ways that she believed to be creatively different from the industry norms. A different dynamic is raised in Case 15, "Colleagues or Sloths? Collaboration and the Allocation of Credit for Contribution," where a colleague was frustrated as she coordinated a project for her peers who subsequently failed to meet the expectations they had agreed to at the start. In Case 16, "Sandy Shores Care Center: A Long-Term Care Staffing Crisis," the idea of recruiting and incentivizing employees is revisited. A care facility leader had limited resources to entice workers to stay and needed new ideas.

Case Preparation and Analysis for Students

Gina Vega and Rob Edwards

> It is not that I'm so smart. But I stay with the questions much longer.
>
> – Albert Einstein

Why Are You in this Class?

Perhaps you are focusing your studies on challenges specific to managerial skills. Perhaps you are taking this class as an elective. Maybe you are a business major who wants to learn a bit more about the issues faced by managers. Maybe this class was the only one open that fits into your schedule.

None of that matters. What does matter is your willingness to participate in your own learning, rather than wait for someone to *tell* you what to learn.

What to Expect from a Case-Based Class

If you are used to a traditional lecture format class, a case class will be a big change for you.

In a traditional class, you are the recipient of knowledge. The instructor is the giver of knowledge, and you receive her words of wisdom passively.

In a case class, you are the creator of knowledge and the discoverer of insights. The instructor is your guide and your facilitator, and she shares in the creation and discovery processes with you.

In a traditional class, the instructor works hard, and you sit quietly. You can send in a tape recorder and listen to the lecture later. You can watch a video and play computer games. You can check your email. You can update your Facebook account.

In a case class, you both work hard and are very much present. You are alert the whole time, because you are responsible for your learning and the learning processes of your classmates. Case learning is social learning and requires active involvement.

Here's how it works:

- You read the assigned case ahead of class. You might consider trying the Three Reads Model in Appendix 0.1 below.

    - Take notes as to the individuals involved, the situations presented, and any connections you can make to theory or analogous characters or situations you have been exposed to before, either in classes or in your work or life experience.

DOI: 10.4324/9781003326298-2

- Identify your assumptions and the information that is missing for you to do a thorough analysis.
- List the problems and select one problem to focus on at a time. Most cases present multiple problems; your ability to identify a key problem will give your case analysis structure and meaning.
- Do any preliminary analysis you can, such as financial comparisons and ratios, statistical analyses or other quantitative explorations. If your analysis is to be qualitative, determine the foundation of your analysis and articulate reasons for and against a strategy or position.
- Write down as many possible recommendations as you can, then select one and commit to it.

- Go to class and get ready for an engaged discussion.

  - The instructor may start off with a précis of the case (or ask you to provide one) and then toss out some icebreaker questions – easy questions to get the conversation moving.
  - The instructor may continue to toss questions to the group or, depending on personal style, may ask questions or opinions directly of one individual.
  - The instructor will tease out a series of analyses, decision-making perspectives, and positions from the class members
  - The class reaches a conclusion, recommendation, decision, or final analysis.

- You may be assigned to a team.

  - If you have been assigned to a case team before the classroom discussion, your preparation should take place with this team.
  - You can expect a lot of lively discussion during the preparation phase, and you will generally (but not always) come to agreement before class.
  - The class discussion will be between team positions rather than individual positions and will proceed as above.

Hints for success in a case class:

- Be prepared.
- Participate actively.
- Allow your emotions to become involved along with your critical analysis.
- Respect your peers' input.
- Try to understand the alternative perspectives put forth in the classroom.
- If on a team, be a "good" team member – no one likes a free rider.

Two Different Types of Cases

There are two different kinds of cases: decision-based cases and descriptive or illustrative cases (Table 0.1).

Table 0.1 Types of cases.

	Decision-based cases	Descriptive or illustrative cases
Description	Decision-based cases will require you to make a reasoned recommendation, supported by facts and theory, for the case protagonist to follow.	Descriptive or illustrative cases do not conclude with a call for a recommendation. Instead, they present a situation that has occurred and your job is to analyze the protagonist's actions.
Example	Your recommendation might be for the protagonist to seek alternative sources of funding rather than depending on friends and family. Some sources he might consider include a bank line of credit, loans, or angel investors. These three sources involve less emotional investment and more straightforward financial analysis to convince lenders.	You may determine that she should have taken a different set of action steps that might have led to a better outcome. Or you may decide that the actions taken were justified and provided the best outcomes under the existing circumstances. Or, your recommendation might be to take advantage of a favorable economy to expand now rather than waiting until the company has accumulated more assets. Even though the protagonist tends to be conservative in his approach to expansion, it makes sense to exploit opportunities that present themselves. It may be a less secure position to take, but the potential rewards may be greater.

In either kind of case, your job will be clear to you, if not from the narrative, then from the questions that follow the case. Be sure to read and think about those questions and use them as guidance in your analysis.

Preparing a Written Case Analysis

The cases in this book are short, designed specifically to help you focus on the key aspects of problems presented. You will, of course, find information in the cases that is not directly relevant to the main problem. Pay attention to this information, as it is likely to be important in your analysis. However, it will not drive your analysis, which should be focused, instead, on the topical components presented in each case.

The analysis of a full-length case can be expected to take a significant amount of time to complete. The analysis of a short case should be, by its nature, short. It will contain all (or most) of the elements described below, but the elements will be short and concise. It is likely that your analysis will include answers to (or take direction from) the questions at the end of the case.

Although it may sound easy to write a short case analysis, do not allow yourself to be tricked into thinking that such an analysis is a snap to put together. It requires discipline to write concisely and to explain complex concepts using simple, clear language. That will be your challenge throughout this course. The examples included in this chapter are based on finance; your cases will likely have a different focus.

Written Analysis of a Short Decision-Based Finance Case

If you are preparing for a class discussion, the Three Reads Method mentioned above will suffice. However, if you have been assigned a **written analysis of a decision-based** case, it can be hard to know where to start. The following model can help you complete a clear and organized decision-based analysis. You can generally use tables, formulas, or matrices instead of narrative sentences if they will support your analysis better.

1. *Executive summary*: Write this section last even though it appears first in the case analysis. The goal of the executive summary is to provide a **brief** overview of the main issues, the proposed recommendation, and the actions to follow. *(2 or 3 sentences)*
2. *Statement of the problem*: Describe the core problem(s) of the case and the decision(s) to be made by the protagonist. Include the symptoms of the problem (s) and differentiate them from the problem(s) themselves. For example, the spots on your face are a symptom. The problem is that you have the measles (or acne, or an allergy to some skin product, or some other infection). This statement of the problem is a **diagnostic process**, and you need to build the rationale for your diagnosis into this section. *(2 or 3 sentences)*
3. *Causes*: This section is an exploration and discussion of potential causes of the main case problem(s). Support your exploration by the application of relevant theories from this course or others. Be sure to use analytical tools that will support your decision-making process and will illustrate your analysis. *(2 or 3 sentences)*
4. *Possible solutions/alternatives*: Surface as many possible solutions or alternative actions as you can. You should not limit your possibilities to what you think is easy to accomplish or logical, but rather entertain a wide variety of options. You do not have to recommend all of these options, but you need to make your instructor aware that you have considered them. *(2 or 3 sentences)*
5. *Selection of criteria and analysis of alternatives*: Select the criteria for determining the basic feasibility of the alternatives identified above. These criteria will guide you in considering the pros and cons of each feasible alternative. Consider at least three alternatives in this section. Sometimes, a tabular format will keep this section organized and clear. You should be prepared to provide financial analyses in this section. *(2 or 3 sentences or small matrix)*
6. *Recommendation*: What do you recommend that the protagonist do? Support your recommendation with a rationale that is based both in facts and in the appropriate theory for the problem (*i.e.*, market analysis, financial statements analysis, the impact of organizational structure, supply chain management, or other disciplinary focus). *(2 or 3 sentences)*
7. *Implementation*: Your instructor may state that no case analysis is complete without providing the action steps to implement the recommendation. What steps should the protagonist take in order to make your recommendation happen? Identify to the greatest extent possible the responsibilities, costs, timeline, and measurement of success of the final implementation.

Appendix 0.2 provides a sample written analysis of a short decision case.

Written Analysis of a Short Descriptive or Illustrative Finance Case

If you are preparing for a class discussion, the method mentioned above or the Three Reads Method at the end of the chapter will suffice. However, if you have been assigned a **written analysis of a descriptive or illustrative finance case**, it can be hard to know where to start. The following model can help you complete a clear and organized analysis. You can generally use tables, formulas, or matrices instead of narrative sentences if they will support your analysis better.

1. *Executive summary*: Write this section last even though it appears first in the case analysis. The goal of the executive summary is to provide a **brief** overview of the main issues, your analysis, and your conclusions. *(2 or 3 sentences)*
2. *The facts*: This is not simply a list of case facts. You need to determine which facts are relevant and which are simply background information or environmental "noise". If you are analyzing a business ethics case, for example, it probably does not matter that the action takes place in the fall. However, in a finance case it may well matter that the action occurs at the end of a sales period, a fiscal year, or at some other critical period. Draw facts not only from the case narrative but, notably, from the exhibits, attachments, financial records, spreadsheets, and other sources within the case. Be sure to peruse these figures carefully for possible errors, misinterpretations, and potential clues to case solutions. *(bulleted list)*
3. *Inferences to be drawn*: Why did things happen as they did? What else might happen as a consequence? What are the implications of these actions in terms of attitudes and relationships? Financial decisions, especially in entrepreneurial environments, are rarely based solely on the numbers. Numbers are generally rational; people rarely are, and their decisions reflect this. *(2 or 3 sentences)*
4. *Theory- and technique-based discussion of the case action*: Apply relevant theory and financial analysis techniques to an explanation of actions and consequences, implications of actions and consequences, and the impact of various outcome criteria on the decisions that were made in the case. The true value of learning entrepreneurial finance lies in the use of actual data to guide future decisions and to draw sensible conclusions about potential outcomes. The financial analyses help you look to the future as well as reflect on the past. *(2 or 3 sentences)*
5. *Options to the actions within the case*: Compare the actions of the protagonist with the other courses of action that were open at the time. What might have been the logical outcomes of those actions? Determine a hierarchy of preferred actions based on outcome criteria you established in step 4 above. *(tabular format)*
6. *Conclusion/Reflection*: This is your rationale for preferred action. If the protagonist has done the right thing according to your analysis, explain why. If the protagonist should have done something else, explain why. Reflect on your reasoning. In a descriptive or illustrative case, your reflection is often the most valuable section because it is from these reflections that future courses of action will derive. *(2 or 3 sentences)*

Appendix 0.3 provides a sample written analysis of a short descriptive case.

How Will Your Written Case Analysis Be Evaluated?

Because case evaluation can be highly subjective, many instructors will prepare a rubric for you to measure your own work against. You can find a basic rubric that outlines generic instructor's expectations and clarifies the standard you should be aiming for in Appendix 0.4. Each instructor's rubric is unique, but the generic rubric provides some guidelines for you to follow.

Appendix 0.5 is a self-grading rubric to help you check your own work for completeness before submission. This self-grader will help to keep you "honest."

Appendix 0.1: Preparing for a Case Discussion – The Three Reads Model for a Short Case

Reading and preparing a case for class discussion involves more than reading a blog, your email, a novel, or a chapter in a textbook. You can develop your case reading skills through the technique outlined below. This technique allows you to make the best possible contribution during the class case discussion. It requires you to read the case (even short cases) three times, twice briefly and once extensively. If you are working with a team, you will want to adapt this process to assure topical coverage.

First Read

- Find six minutes (yes, six minutes is enough for the one-to-four-page cases in this book) to sit down uninterrupted. Mute your phone so that you do not get distracted during this short reading period.
- Read the hook. This may be several paragraphs long in a full-length case, but just one or two sentences in the cases in this book. The hook will introduce you to the case "problem." Jot down the problem in the margin.
- Read the first sentence (and only the first sentence) of each paragraph in the case. Write a keyword or two in the margin next to the paragraph.
- Read the titles only of any attachments and exhibits.
- Turn your phone back on and go about your business.

Second Read

- This is the big one – a two-page case will take you at least 30 minutes. Remember that if you have interruptions, this period must be extended.
- Read the entire case, slowly and carefully. Jot notes as you go along about the characters and their behavior, the situation and the action. Sometimes preparing a timeline of action makes it easier to follow and remember. Be sure to include any exhibits and attachments during this read.
- Jot down your own response to the situation and the characters, even if it's unsupported by theories or formal concepts. Make any connections you can to analogous situations you have experienced or read about. What are the differences or similarities to this situation? Remember, these notes that you are making are yours alone – no one else will be looking at them. It doesn't matter if they are messy, have lines drawn all over them, are put together in right-brain or left-brain style, just as long as they exist. They are meant to help you.
- Make a list of the assumptions you are making, the financial analyses you need to conduct, and the information you still need before you make a recommendation. Something is always missing, or the case would be really boring. So, what is missing?
- List the alternative solutions to the case, their pros and cons, and then select one recommendation. You always have to commit to one recommendation and

provide a rationale for it. This recommendation should be supported by theory, experience, quantitative analysis, or other rationale.

- Prepare any case questions you have been assigned. Be sure to check any spreadsheets for errors or misinterpretations.
- You should be tired at this point. Put the case away.

Third Read

- This last read takes place not too long before class. The point of it is to make sure that the case is fresh in your mind and that you are still comfortable with your recommendation.
- This read resembles the first read: read the beginning, the first sentence of each paragraph, etc. But this time, include both your marginal notes and the notes you have made during the second read. You will need these notes to participate actively in class. Remember that class participation means that you have to talk – it's OK to read aloud what you have written if you are uncomfortable talking off the cuff.
- The entire process has taken two hours or less, which is about two thirds the amount of time you should anticipate using for class preparation for a 1½ hour class. If your class period is longer than this, your preparation should be commensurately more extensive.

Appendix 0.2: Sample Written Case Analysis for a Short Decision-Based Finance Case

This abbreviated analysis was prepared from M. Lam & R. Luther, "The Offer Price," *The CASE Journal*, vol. 8.2 (2012).

Executive Summary

Koehler Propane was a small, family-owned propane dealer with a very small heating oil division inherited through a prior acquisition. A local heating oil dealer was put up for sale and Koehler had to decide whether or not to purchase it, and if so, at what price and on what terms. The best strategy for Koehler is to offer a cash price of between $800,000 and $850,000.

Statement of the Problem

The propane and heating oil dealer industry was in the declining phase of its life cycle and was characterized by high fluctuations in revenue due to uncertainty in energy prices and weather, high fixed-assets requirement and regulations by both federal and state agencies. Competition was high and business growth either involved intense price competition or acquisition of competing companies. Koehler and his son had to decide whether to buy the heating oil company or to close down their own small heating oil division altogether.

Causes

Some of Koehler's current equipment needed replacement if he were to remain in the heating oil business. Koehler had an advantage over competing bidders in a cash deal but not in a stock deal. The four valuation methods (discounted cash flow valuation and multiples valuation, multiples valuation, EBITDA multiple method, and percent of annual sales + inventory method) range from $624,019 to $918,606, averaging $818,469. A reasonable cash price ranged from $800,000 to $850,000.

Possible Solutions/Alternatives

Koehler Propane had three alternatives:

- Close down the oil business: Closing down the heating oil business would eliminate a break-even/money-losing division and allow Koehler to stay focused on its core business of propane delivery but it would be contrary to their vision of developing Koehler into a large energy company.
- Purchase two new trucks to replace existing ones: Purchasing new trucks required capital investments into a potentially money losing division. Given the low volume and the surcharge they had to pay due to lack of bulk storage, they were at a cost disadvantage, severely limiting their ability to compete on price.
- Acquire the heating oil company: This would advance Koehler toward a more diverse product line and increase the size of its business. It would provide Koehler bulk storage facilities and make them a major heating oil distributor in the vicinity. If Koehler failed to acquire the heating oil company, one of its competitors would gain entrance into its primary territory and Koehler would face increased competition in its propane business.

Selection of Criteria and Analysis of Alternatives

Note that the assignment of values for the three alternatives is arbitrary and meant as an example only. You would assign values as relevant for your own analysis (see Table 0.2).

Recommendation

Closing down the oil business is bad for growth, for diversification, and for capital investment. If quantified, the option has 0 value. Purchasing two new trucks is good for capital investment, but "iffy" for both growth and diversification. If quantified, the option has a potential value of 30+. Acquiring the heating oil company is good for growth, diversification, and capital investment. Quantified, the option has a potential value of 100.

Both companies are located in the same town, and the two owners have past business relationships, therefore Koehler will have better knowledge of the oil company than competing bidders. Competing bidders may be unwilling to offer a cash deal, or they will likely offer a much lower cash price. Koehler has an advantage over competing bidders in a cash deal but not in a stock deal. Given the advantages of a cash deal to the oil company, the best strategy for Koehler is to offer a cash price.

Table 0.2 Selection of criteria and analysis of alternatives.

Criterion	Assigned value	Pro	Con
Growth	40	They want to be industry leaders, larger customer base	Declining industry, high competition
Diversification	30	One of the main business goals	High risk, expensive
Capital investment	30	More dependable equipment	Potential dedication of needed cash to non-liquid assets

Implementation

1. Agree on a valuation.
2. Structure the deal internally.
3. Negotiate with the seller for a mutually agreeable acquisition.

Appendix 0.3: Sample Written Case Analysis for a Short Descriptive/ Illustrative Finance Case

This abbreviated analysis was prepared from G. Vega & M. Lam, "Howling Wolf Taqueria: Feeding the Good Wolf," *Case Research Journal*, vol. 34, issue 2 (2013).

1. **Executive summary**: A schoolteacher has decided to open a taqueria in a small, historic New England city. The problem is whether he should launch his business at the time of the case in light of the many challenges facing him. He could not provide all the necessary information and was reluctant to listen to advice. He should not launch his business at this time.
2. **The facts**: The entrepreneur knew a little bit about a lot of things, but not enough about any one of the functional elements of his business to run it on his own. He had insufficient funds to last through a dry spell; he was being pushed to launch because the landlord of his desired location was in a hurry to get the lease signed. He did not have a full liquor license. Money was tight, loans were non-existent, and his debt to asset ratio did not approach the industry standard. It also looks like he needs to do a closer examination of his anticipated revenues.
3. **Inferences to be drawn**: The Howling Wolf is likely to create value for the customer, as there appears to be growing demand for this type of cuisine and there is little direct competition. However, the money-making potential of the restaurant is unclear, and the owner's ability to sustain operations with the proposed family/ friends staff is doubtful. A launch would be a high risk/minimal reward strategy.
4. **Theory- and technique-based discussion of the case action**: A SWOT analysis showed that he had some significant strengths and opportunities in terms of personal contacts and an opening in the restaurant market. His passion, product and service differentiation, and personal skills suggest that he can provide an appealing venue for locals to enjoy a unique culinary experience. Potential funders have not been found, the economy is weak (although beginning to rebound slightly), and money is scarce. Although the entrepreneur believes strongly in his restaurant, he has been unable to provide financials that support that belief for banks or other funders. Computing breakeven revenue and cash burn rate show that breakeven weekly revenue is 4.35% below the original estimate. Total monthly cash outflow excluding COGS is over $34k compared to a beginning cash balance of only $61k. If revenue is more than 23% below the original estimate, he will run out of cash in 6 months.
5. **Options to the actions within the case**. Decision criteria: Potential to make a good return. Likelihood of staying in business without a liquor license. Potential to survive on limited investment. Likelihood of family and friends to continue providing low-cost assistance. The entrepreneur has to weight the importance of each of the decision criteria before making his decision. There are two possible decisions that the entrepreneur could take:

- The entrepreneur could open based on the support that he had from his family and his experience with this type of cuisine and confidence that the tourist season would likely be able to cover the slow season
- The entrepreneur could postpone opening until acquiring more funds, a liquor license, and business advisors

Conclusion/reflection. Based on the analyses above, I would not recommend launching the business at this time. I think the entrepreneur should find an angel or other investor to provide the financial stability that will cover him through the tough times during the first year of operations. He should continue his efforts to obtain a full liquor license. He should plan to invest in advertising prior to his launch, and he should conduct a full-scale location analysis prior to signing his lease.

Appendix 0.4: Generic Grading Rubric

How Will My Written Case Analysis Be Evaluated?

Because evaluation can be highly subjective, many instructors will prepare a rubric for you to measure your own work against. This rubric outlines the instructor's expectations and clarifies the standard you should be aiming for. Each instructor's rubric is unique, but the generic rubric that follows provides some guidelines for you to follow.

Table 0.3 Case analysis evaluation.

Suggested criteria	Poor, weak, needs improvement	Satisfactory, acceptable, good	Outstanding, exemplary, excellent
Thoroughness	One or more required section is missing or treated perfunctorily X points	All required sections are addressed to a great extent X points	All required sections are addressed completely X points
Theoretical relevance	The analysis does not incorporate relevant theories X points	Addresses theories and course concepts appropriately X points	Addresses theories and concepts appropriately and insightfully X points
Quality of analysis	Does not suggest careful thought or provide insights X points	Analysis suggests both effort and understanding of the material X points	Detailed analysis that offers careful and logical inferences X points
Conclusions or implementation	Unsupported or missing arguments overlook salient issues X points	Supported arguments capture main issues X points	Supported arguments address both main issues and subtle or secondary problems X points
Writing quality	Careless writing, many grammar and spelling errors, poor organization X points	Clear writing, few grammar and spelling errors, organized presentation X points	Flawless writing, clear organization, correct grammar and spelling X points

Appendix 0.5: Self-Grading Rubric

Use this rubric to evaluate the quality of your own work before you hand it in.

Table 0.4 Self-grading rubric.

	Something is wrong	Everything is correct	Student comment here
Presence of all required elements (refer to original assignment)	What is missing? Add it.	In the column to the right, list the items that appear in the Table of Contents.	
Issues	Some primary or secondary issues are missing.	All the primary and secondary issues have been dealt with and prioritized.	
Adequacy of discussion of consequences, depth of data analysis, application of theory	Weak in one or more of the listed areas.	Issues are fully developed, including alternatives, consequences clearly spelled out, data analysis is comprehensive, and theory is applied correctly	
Quality of expression	I have not run Spellcheck or Grammarcheck. I have not had someone else proofread my work.	My work has been proofread by someone else and all errors have been corrected.	
Would I be willing to turn in this report to my employer?	If no – fix it!	If yes, you're done. Hand it in.	
What grade would you give this project?	C or less	A or B	

Part I

Creating a Positive Climate and Organizational Culture

Introduction

The four cases in Part I introduce managerial challenges around creating an inclusive workplace climate that encourages employee engagement. Case 1 follows a manager who joins an existing team and realizes that several benefits could result if she gained her employees' trust and got them to share their job knowledge with her and each other. Case 2 similarly deals with a new manager, who was also the new owner of the café. Her vision necessitated the creation of trust and rebuilding the company culture from the ground up. Case 3 provides an example of a psychologically safe climate in which employees can trust managers who learn about their mistakes. In contrast, Case 4 presents the situation of a third-party contractor whose experience with the company culture is that of a perceived outsider. The questions and readings below build on these themes of leadership, trust, psychological safety, and organizational culture.

Part I Cases

Case 1, "Quiet Springs: Engaging Your Team as a New Leader," illustrates some of the challenges that come with assuming a supervisory position of an intact group as a new member of an organization. When Ava Lehrer joined Quiet Springs Inc. as a manager, she was faced with a group of individuals who seemed variably skeptical and hesitant to trust her and each other, and unwilling to share information and knowledge. Ava enacted several practices to influence a new work unit culture.

The learning objectives for this case include:

- Associate the practices of observation, empathy, individualized attention, and goal-setting to a new manager's effective onboarding within a work unit.
- Explain the importance of fostering a culture where employees appreciate open sharing of knowledge and continuous learning.
- Identify positive outcomes of attentive management, such as feelings of safety, empowerment, cohesiveness, and engagement.

Case 2, "Building a (New) Company Culture at Ma Reilly's Café," focuses on a complete takeover and transformation of a prior business under a different name. This case follows the challenges that new owners have in buying a small café and trying to transform the failing business with a laissez-fair owner to one with a positive organizational culture and a supportive and hands-on management approach that involved coaching. Linda Kokoros and her husband purchased the café, received brief and limited training, and faced a staff that had previously received minimal supervision or coaching.

DOI: 10.4324/9781003326298-4

The learning objectives for this case include:

- Identify the aspects of an organization's culture that are easier or more difficult to change.
- Analyze how leaders and their approaches can influence an organization's culture.

Case 3, "Reveal a Mistake to the Boss? Trust and Psychological Safety in a Market Research Team," reveals a data science team lead's need to deal with an employee's error. The data science team was comprised of three individuals who had collaborative, supportive relationships with one another, and mistakes were rare. They were part of the research division at a global market research firm. The data science team did not work with clients, but instead wrote code that client-facing teams utilized. In this case, one of the data scientists, Sean, made a mistake in his code which was then used by a client-focused team to create reports and presentations to an important client that the company had hoped would lead to additional clients in the future. When the data scientist realized his mistake, he reached out to his team lead, Chirag. Chirag had to decide how to address the mistake/failure with the individual and with the team in ways that maintained trust and a psychologically safe environment.

The learning objectives for this case include:

- Identify the relevant factors for creating a psychologically safe team environment.
- Assess how to maintain such an environment in a sensitive situation.
- Recognize the opportunity for failure to facilitate learning.

Case 4, "The Outspoken Contractor: Inclusion and Conflict Across Organizational Boundaries," takes the viewpoint of a manager of contract employees who faced yet another instance of the ongoing conflict between full-time workers and contract workers. The challenge is to understand the organizational culture and other structural causes of the conflict and what might be done to avoid such problems in the future.

The learning objectives for this case include:

- Identify the type and organizational sources of conflict in a workplace situation.
- Develop recommendations for a manager to minimize conflict and group differences between full-time and contract workers.
- Utilize effective negotiation strategies to resolve a conflict situation.

Part I Supplemental Questions

Reflection Questions

1. Describe the different styles/approaches of two leaders with whom you have volunteered or worked in the past. Which style did you like best, and why?
2. Have you ever experienced leadership turnover in a job, volunteer position, sports organization, or other group to which you belonged? What behaviors of the new leader or aspects of the situation made that transition more difficult for you or others? What aspects of the situation or leader actions made the transition less difficult?

Discussion Questions

1. What questions might a job applicant ask to discern if employees have a sense of psychological safety and trust their manager?
2. How might a new manager gain and foster employees' trust?
3. How does an organization's culture relate to the ways in which workplace conflict is handled?
4. What challenges might part-time or temporary workers face when it comes to being trusted by managers (or trusting them) and being integrated into an organization's workplace culture?

Part I Related Readings and Video

Transformational Leadership and Organizational Culture

Agarwal, P. (2018). How to create a positive workplace culture. Accessed at: www.forbes.com/sites/pragyagarwaleurope/2018/08/29/how-to-create-a-positive-work-place-culture/?sh=525d01264272

Ugochukwu, C. (2024). Transformational leadership style: How to inspire and motivate. Accessed at: www.simplypsychology.org/what-is-transformational-leadership.html

Psychological Safety in the Workplace

APA. (2023). What is psychological safety at work? Here's how to start creating it. Accessed at: www.apa.org/topics/healthy-workplaces/psychological-safety

Edmondson, A. (2014). Building a psychologically safe workplace. Accessed at: www.youtube.com/watch?v=LhoLuui9gX8

Ravishankar, R. A. (2022). A guide to building psychological safety on your team. *Harvard Business Review*, December 1. Accessed at: https://hbr.org/2022/12/a-guide-to-building-psychological-safety-on-your-team

Trust and Leaders

Civitella, A. (2019). How to build trust as a leader. Accessed at: www.forbes.com/sites/forbescoachescouncil/2019/05/07/how-to-build-trust-as-a-leader

Covey, S. M. (2009). How the best leaders build trust. Accessed at: www.shrm.org/topics-tools/news/organizational-employee-development/how-best-leaders-build-trust

Frei, F. X. & Morriss, A. (2020). Begin with trust: The first step to becoming a genuinely empowering leader. *Harvard Business Review*, May–June. Accessed at: https://hbr.org/2020/05/begin-with-trust

Case 1   Quiet Springs

Engaging Your Team as a New Leader

Quinn W. Cunningham, Apryl L. Roach and Eugene J. Kutcher

Synopsis

When Ava Lehrer joined Quiet Springs Inc., she was faced with a group of individuals who seemed variably skeptical and hesitant to trust her and each other, and unwilling to share information and knowledge. Ava enacted several practices to influence a new work unit culture.

Ava Lehrer recently joined Quiet Springs Inc. as their Director of Operations. She was hired to lead a cross-functional group of warehouse and customer service employees who were tasked with coordinating the production of their two main product lines. These employees included Charlie, the warehouse receiver, Logan, the forklift operator, Jamie, in production, Morgan, a purchaser, and Blake from customer service. Arriving on her first day, Ava energetically told her team, "I am very much looking forward to working with you! I hope to be someone you all feel comfortable approaching and talking with and I look forward to our team growing and developing together!"

In her first three weeks, Ava made several concerning observations about how employees worked together. For example, Charlie appeared disinterested in sharing details of his work experiences with Ava, and Jamie would consistently withhold ideas from the group, but later share them privately with Ava. When Ava tried to work with the group to brainstorm ways to make their collaboration more effective, no one would engage.

As Ava reflected on the situation, she noted a few things. Charlie was a member of the Shipping and Receiving department. As a receiver, his priorities were making sure that everything was unloaded from the delivery trucks and that the materials were checked in the same day. During their first one-on-one meeting, Ava asked Charlie about how he did this work. Charlie hesitated and seemed visibly uncomfortable. He replied, "Look, I complete my tasks, I do a good job, isn't that all that really matters? I don't really want to have to go through everything I do each day." Ava tried to probe for more answers: "Do you feel like you've had the proper training for your work?" "Yes," replied Charlie. "Do you feel like you all have the resources you need to do your job?" Ava asked. "I don't know," Charlie answered rather curtly. Ava wasn't sure if she should consider this insubordinate behavior, but she was still in the "getting to know you" phase with her employees and didn't want to jump to any premature conclusions.

DOI: 10.4324/9781003326298-5

Logan had been a forklift driver for a few years before Ava arrived. As part of the Shipping and Receiving department, he worked closely with Charlie. Logan talked a lot about making sure shipments were unloaded from trucks quickly and either moved to the production floor or stocked in an efficient manner. He told Ava, "I need to have Charlie helping me stock parts; no one else knows how to do it right. If Charlie can't help me, then he or I are just gonna end up having to fix whatever anyone else does. If I can't get Charlie's help, we will end up with a backlog of parts on the warehouse floor, I can promise you that."

Jamie was the production manager and was very focused on ensuring that product parts arrived on time and were brought to the production floor for product assembly. Jamie seemed to be one of the last people to leave the office each day, as she was repeatedly cross-checking arrival dates for parts and comparing those dates with customer delivery dates. On one occasion, Jamie arrived to work looking incredibly sick and when Ava suggested she return home, Jamie said, "I can't go home; what if I need time off later in the year? I can't take time off now." Ava tried once more to convince Jamie to go home to no avail. Instead, Jamie insisted on staying at work until she had all the parts prepared for the next day's production line.

Morgan was in Purchasing and her main priority was ensuring that all the parts needed to build products were in stock and ready for assembly. She communicated with external vendors on a regular basis and provided updates to the rest of the team if and when there were going to be delays. She also interacted with Jamie quite a bit to stay aware of schedules and deadlines to determine if the required parts were all in stock.

Finally, Blake was a customer service representative and interacted with clients daily. While she could choose to ask any of her teammates about updates on parts, assembly, and shipping dates, Ava noticed that Blake tended to reach out only to Morgan. Sometimes, this meant Morgan had to reach out to Charlie, Jamie, or Logan to get updates from them to then report their answers back to Blake. Ava noticed that when Blake had no choice but to interact with Charlie, Jamie, or Logan, she seemed to be somewhat curt. Ava wondered if there had been problems among them in the past.

Starting a New Managerial Position

Quiet Springs had been in the office furniture manufacturing business for about 20 years and prided themselves on creating ergonomic furniture that makes working life healthier and more efficient. Their main product lines were a desk chair and a convertible standing desk, though they produced other items like bookcases, conference table sets, and breakroom cabinetry.

Ava arrived at Quiet Springs with an MBA degree and a little under 20 years of experience as a supervisor, manager, and director at other companies. She had been excited for this opportunity, but entered unfamiliar territory as it was her first time in a high-end corporate furnishings company and in the manufacturing sector. Her prior experience had mainly been in non-profit human resources. In addition, Ava was replacing a manager who had been with Quiet Springs for over a decade. Ava could tell that their management styles were different, and that as a newcomer, she needed to find ways to bond with her employees and develop their trust.

Shortly after arriving, Ava learned that the previous manager did not require documentation about operational processes and had also struggled to help employees develop new systems or techniques for their work. She was surprised that, at minimum, there wasn't an operations manual for each department. She wondered how anything was supposed to get done if an employee was sick or on vacation. She saw the consequences of such a gap when Charlie was absent for two days and there was no plan for how to get his work done; although Logan could physically move the parts off the delivery trucks, he couldn't check these parts into the computer system so that they could be used for assembly. After getting to know her employees better over the first few months, Ava discovered that they had not been trained beyond the initial instructions they received from previous employees, and had difficulty explaining what had, over time, become tacit knowledge.

Ava decided to focus on setting immediate and short-term goals. Her immediate goals were to read the employee handbook and observe and analyze the culture of the organization. Her short-term goals included meeting with each employee to get to know them as individuals and to learn about their day-to-day work. She was interested in making their time at work more enjoyable, in identifying knowledge gaps, and in ultimately transitioning her team into one that was more focused on fostering a learning environment.

Ava understood that a few things were critical to helping her team become more effective. She needed to: (1) understand the current state of relative knowledge among her team of employees, (2) envision a concrete plan of how this team could function when the employees were better aligned with one another, (3) perform an audit of the departments in order to identify interdependencies and available technological resources, and (4) create departmental-level plans for knowledge and skill development.

To begin a conversation among her employees, Ava asked them for their opinions and feelings about the current state of knowledge management. She wanted her employees to feel empowered to provide input in how the current system could be improved. In her email, she wrote, "I would like to meet with each of you individually so that I can get to know you so that you can help in my new role. Yes, I am the manager, but you are the expert in your particular work function and the best person to share this information with me." She met with each employee individually to learn about their time so far at Quiet Springs, and what they understood about their current role and responsibilities. She also asked each employee to reflect on whether there was anything she could do to improve their work experience, be it something that would make them feel more comfortable at the office or any supplies that would help them be more productive. Example requests included multicolored Post-It notes for Jamie and a wireless telephone headset for Blake.

Knowledge Management

While meeting with each employee, Ava noticed a trend: it seemed her employees felt very little job security and thus did not want to disclose their working processes and procedures. Jamie told Ava, "If I create a document that lists everything I do, then someone else will be able to just step in and do my job, and then what reason do they have to keep me? They could fire me at any moment and replace me with someone they can pay less." Charlie had a similar sentiment and told Ava that he really didn't feel comfortable writing up his processes and procedures both because (1) it would take a long time and (2) someone else could too easily take over his job. Ava decided she needed to take a step back and help her employees understand why she was asking them to document their work tasks. She asked them to recall a time when they had taken a vacation from work or had been home due to illness and then they had to return to days (or weeks) worth of work that had piled up while they were away. She told them, "If we have a knowledge management system, with details of what you do every day, then while you are out sick or on vacation, another worker can temporarily continue to do the work, and then you could return with minimal backed-up work to deal with."

As her employees started to better understand that having documented processes was considered a "best practice" in most organizations, they became less resistant to the idea of writing down all of the things they did on a regular basis. Ava explained that in her role as manager, she needed the ability to make sure the business was always operational and that she was counting on their knowledge, skills, and abilities to come together. She expressed how she needed them to meet her in the middle as a team so they could collectively own this goal of shared knowledge. Knowing that Ava was there for them, and would advocate on their behalf, they began to cooperate. One day, Ava overheard Morgan and Jamie discussing what to include in the resource binder that would contain their day-to-day functions and operations. Ava was also happy to see Blake engaging directly with Charlie and making an effort to understand how the receiving process works and why deliveries might be delayed on their way to the production floor. Delays in the production process had apparently been one of Blake's frustrations as she was the one who had to let the customer know when shipments were delayed. She did not enjoy having to give customers bad news when she thought the products should have been able to be assembled on time. In talking with Charlie, she picked up on some of the nuanced production issues and began brainstorming ways to streamline that process.

Time Off from Work

Ava also noticed in her first few months at Quiet Springs that her employees seemed rather reluctant to request time off. Morgan poked her head into Ava's office one day to ask, "Would it be okay for me to take a day off on Thursday? My spouse has a last-minute work trip and I don't have any childcare." Ava was surprised by the way Morgan asked the question, as though Morgan did not feel like she was permitted to take time off to deal with legitimate family issues. Another day, Jamie timidly asked Ava, "Do you mind if I take a half day on Friday?" Ava was mindful to use these opportunities to reinforce her support of her employees. She replied to both, "I will always say 'yes' unless there is a business reason I need to say 'no.' Regardless, your health and family always come first." In an effort to encourage her employees to not feel apprehensive when requesting time off, Ava told her them to send her an email with their time off request and she would send the approval to their Outlook calendars.

Conclusion

Ava was excited for the new challenges she was encountering at Quiet Springs. She realized that her external perspective was helping the group develop in new ways. While her plans had been put in motion, there was still much work to do. She recognized that maintaining this level of trust and continuing to enhance complex outcomes like individual attitudes and team culture would take ongoing work. How might Ava ensure that the employees will not fall back into old habits? What other short-term goals should she be considering, such as something related to encouraging the development of learning mindsets among her employees? What other long-term goals should she be working on? How can Ava continue to effect positive change?

Reflection Questions

1. Think about a job or volunteer position you've held and identify knowledge about the work you did that was not documented anywhere. How did you come to have that tacit knowledge?
2. Have you ever been in a situation where you had to gain others' trust? What did you do and did your efforts result in them trusting you?

Learning Applications

1. Analyze this situation using two course concepts, frameworks, or models.
2. Identify three key actions that Ava took to change the dynamics in her department. Explain why they were or were not effective.

Supplemental Readings

Prabhakaran, J. (2021). What is tacit knowledge: Importance, benefits & examples. Accessed January 10, 2024 at: https://document360.com/blog/tacit-knowledge/

Utz, J. (2024). Why trust is the currency of product management. Accessed January 10, 2024 at: https://productcoalition.com/why-trust-is-the-currency-of-product-management-a9a24341fbe1

Case 2 Building a (New) Company Culture at Ma Reilly's Café

Laurie L. Levesque and George C. Kokoros

Synopsis

Building a (New) Company Culture at Ma Reilly's Café focuses on a complete takeover and transformation of a prior business under a different name. This case follows the challenges that new owners have in buying a small café and trying to transform the failing business with a laissez-fair owner to one with a positive organizational culture and a supportive and hands-on management approach. Linda Kokoros and her husband purchased the café, received brief and limited training, and faced a staff that have had minimal oversight and training.

Building a New Culture One Interaction at a Time

In the months immediately after purchasing a café, Linda Kokoros, the new co-owner, accepted that there would be some natural attrition as high school employees left for college and when staff had other responsibilities that prevented them from maintaining their part-time job. Most employees eventually adjusted to the approach of the new owners. A few, such as Emily, had not adapted well to the ongoing presence of a manager or the changes in café operations, such as a new friendlier approach to serving customers. Linda's husband George, the other co-owner, was less patient with employee pushback or unwillingness to get on board, especially as the café's transformation had been underway for some months. He encouraged Linda to terminate Emily, the only employee still unwilling to adapt. Linda, however, believed all employees were "coachable."

Buying the Dream

Linda Kokoros had a dream to combine her management expertise with a love of baking learned at home – she wanted to open a café that replicated the community feel in Irish cafés like Bewley's and O'Briens. Linda liked the efficiency of their cafeteria-style service counters with everything made in-house and to order. She was raised in Dublin, Ireland and everyone locally had called Linda's mother "Ma" and in turn, "Ma Reilly" had made everyone feel welcome. Prior to emigrating to the US, Linda managed a production facility where there was great attention to quality and detail, and she also identified and resolved inefficiencies. She coached and guided employees by asking questions that forced them to reflect on what they had done well

DOI: 10.4324/9781003326298-6

or poorly and to identify what they could learn from those insights. She guided or lent a hand as needed to help them succeed. Developing employees was important to keeping production flowing and avoiding turnover. Linda later refined her approach at WW International, Inc. (formerly Weight Watchers) where she "trained coaches who struggled to help customers meet weight loss goals." The coaches disliked most other corporate trainers, because they focused on the coaches' faults. Linda flipped that model and helped coaches build upon their strengths.

Linda's husband, George, had a very different background. George was an American who had worked in several high-growth and startup businesses like Staples and Fortune Brands. He was used to fast-paced decision making and scaling large businesses. Due to those environments, George was experienced in making quick personnel decisions and letting go of staff unable to keep up with rapid growth.

The intent was to build the café by renovating an existing structure, but few properties for sale matched her needs. The Kokoroses found an ideal space on a busy main road in a small city with a back door that opened onto municipal parking. The negotiation for the space ended after its landlord indicated that café customers would not be allowed access to the back door as his trucks would be parked there. Their building contractor had evaluated several other potential café sites, and then told them about a restaurant for sale near where they lived whose owner of 20 years wanted to leave the food service industry. They discussed how renovating an existing restaurant's kitchen and seating area was cost-effective, and less risky than building a restaurant in a new location and needing extensive advertising just to create a new customer base. Renovating also meant initially taking over the existing restaurant – and Linda was not interested in running someone else's business. George worked hard to convince Linda that the cash-flow opportunities of an existing business would provide the runway needed to build her dream.

The Kokoroses decided that a renovation project was the best option to pursue Linda's dream of owning a café. This was new territory as neither had restaurant experience, yet they planned to invest their life savings into it. As anonymous customers they scoped out the location, size, and layout of the restaurant for sale. George realized he had actually had an unmemorable meal there once after their kids' sports game. From driving by, they also knew it was rarely busy. Inside, Linda noticed unused chalkboards for describing specials and a pastry and bread case filled with store bought items. She believed she could turn the place around with on-site baking, excellent service, and a welcoming atmosphere for customers and employees. They went ahead and negotiated the purchase, and agreed to the owner's request that they would not go into the café until the sale was final and the seller had notified her staff. Prior to the Memorial Day holiday in May 2016, they finalized the purchase of the business name, assets, menu, and marketing customer lists. The seller informed her staff and instructed them to come into work as usual the day after the holiday when she would train the new owners on how to run the café. Nancy, a part-timer, was one of a dozen employees shocked by the announcement and a little intimidated as the current owner "knew how we worked. What if this new person doesn't?"

New owners, same business

The doors re-opened after the holiday as if it were the same business – the name, menu, and staff were unchanged. The only difference was that Linda and George Kokoros were onsite. They met the employees and worked alongside them to learn the business. The staff were all part-timers in their early twenties or in high school. George noted, "They greeted us warmly, but we noticed them observing us; I assumed it was to gauge what kind of people we were." The couple deliberately adopted the demeanor that they were "one of the employees, not the owners" during that training period. Over three days, they worked side-by-side with staff and the previous owner who was not forthcoming with information. They had much to learn – how to buy supplies, deal with suppliers, manage inventory, clean, comply with health code rules, fax the daily specials, manage catering orders, and prep and serve coffee and various breakfast items and sandwiches.

The new owners became heavily involved in learning every task; they made coffee and food, answered the phone, prepped food, and more. They cashed out customers with the antiquated push button register, which left them unsure if they had charged incorrect prices. Food orders were handwritten and those slips of paper were walked to the kitchen to be hung on the "clothesline." Linda told the staff she was learning, and that "for now, the menu is the menu, and the specials will continue." George lamented, "[The previous owner] did what she was obligated to do to train us, and said 'you guys can figure this out'." Linda elaborated, "We had the impression that her heart wasn't into managing the business over the last few years. She alienated customers and we realized quickly that it wasn't great to have her at the counter. She was abrasive with customers, and she and George were like oil and water." Linda and George found the first couple of weeks to be eye-opening, "the state of the business that was laid out in negotiations was different from what we found." The staff was unaware of the restaurant's very weak financial position, and that status quo was not viable going forward. For example, staff prepared a lot of coffee in advance to be served from the urns. As the weather warmed, sales transitioned to iced coffee. The new owners noticed that staff didn't adjust their preparation and a great deal of hot coffee was discarded each day without a thought to the cost.

Linda was perplexed by how things were done. She observed, took copious notes, and identified operational changes to make over a 3-, 6-, and 12-month period along with rolling out a new company name and branding. She wanted to fix things quickly, especially inefficiencies. However, she committed to understanding first how the operation worked, thus she made no changes in those first weeks. Customers told George that they "hadn't known what the café's actual hours were." Most staff worked "mothers' hours" (e.g., 10 a.m. to 2 p.m.) and the high school students worked afternoons to do prep for the next day. Two part-time drivers delivered the catering orders. The owner arrived anytime from 9–11 a.m. and "only came out of the office to fill in if she was needed," according to Carrie, who had worked part-time after she got out of school. She noted, "We weren't trained on all aspects, so sometimes we'd go to the office with a question only to find that [the owner] had left without telling us. So, we'd have to guess at the ingredients by reading the menu." In general, the owner was hands-off, so the unwritten rule was that "you had the freedom to do it your way."

Nancy or another employee would open the café and set up using task lists to guide the process. The opener was both cashier and cook. Regardless of how many customers waited, that employee took the order and then went into the back to make the food using printed instructions about what ingredients to use or how to weigh out the meats for various sandwiches. Linda realized the lists were used because "staff hadn't received a lot of direction or leadership" or training. Linda noticed that the staff panicked when there were more than two tickets in the kitchen for food items. They had not been trained well, and there were no processes in place to help them prior-itize and be efficient. George recalled the time a few years prior when he had gone into the café with other dads while their kids were playing a game nearby. They all had ordered egg breakfast sandwiches and coffees. The one employee working in the café took the orders and disappeared into the kitchen for 15 minutes, during which time they stood hoping their orders were being prepared, as the employee didn't interact with them at all during that time. Other customers came in and were not greeted as there were no other employees on the premises. Few customers arrived after lunch, but the café was open until afternoon or early evening whenever the owner decided to close. Shifts dragged by, and the workers reported spending many afternoons sitting on the counters or napping on a bench.

During those first weeks, it was sometimes tense. The staff tended to emulate the former owner's interactions with customers and each other. Tips were not shared, orders were not customized, and some interactions did not feel collegial. Employees like Emily often corrected the new owners, saying, "Oh no, you don't do it that way, that's not how we do it" in response to preparing menu items, coffee, setting up the café and kitchen, and as Linda perceived, "just about everything." Sometimes they corrected the Kokoroses in front of customers, which to Linda felt as if "they had crossed the line" but was in keeping with what had previously been acceptable in the café. Carrie repeatedly asked the former owner, "Can you help Linda and George with ..." and was told, "They have to figure it out for themselves." Carrie "felt helpless" and she "didn't want to see them fail" so she trained them on what little she knew. In doing so, George thought most owners would not tolerate her tone (e.g., "Why did you pick up that coffee cup? We put them over here.") and that she was very hard on him, as he had no prior experience. Linda and George didn't immediately push back as they didn't want anyone to quit, and they truly thought Carrie and most staff were trying to be helpful.

New Owners, New Company Culture

The vision for the new restaurant was initiated when the name changed to "Ma Reilly's Café" as a living tribute to Linda's mother. Though they started with the old menu, Linda planned changes such as baking all pastries, muffins, scones, and Irish soda breads from scratch on premises. Sandwich items remained on the menu, and new items were added. Linda knew how to lead others to create a positive work environment; she needed to get staff to accept new processes and ways of working together. She slowly introduced new ways of doing things, Nancy noticed the changes didn't happen by Linda saying "'Do it because I'm the owner,' but instead by Linda saying things such as, 'We can all benefit from it, just try it.'" From the first, Nancy believed Linda was a good person so she deci-ded to keep working there after the business changed hands. A few employees had left for college or quit to focus on their full-time jobs. Nancy assumed "change was hard for them – and they struggled" after the former owner left and Linda questioned workflow and processes and made suggestions.

Linda and George increasingly asserted more authority. One day a catering delivery driver gave George a hard time. George subsequently called the driver into the office and told, "this is going to be your last day." The driver was dumbfounded; it never crossed his mind that could be an outcome. Although George recanted after a per-formance conversation, the story was shared among staff and it set a new more respectful tone.

Several additional employees were hired to work from 9 a.m. until early afternoon. Linda met her staff each morning to give directions regarding who would do what, and she indicated what she herself would work on, such as food prep, catering orders, and baking. After the day's baking was finished and catering orders prepared, Linda asked her staff "where do you need me?" and then jumped in to help no matter what was needed. She washed dishes, mopped the floor, and did whatever task was asked of her. When she bustled in to assist with whatever employees said they needed help doing, they joked, "The Ma Reilly's Bus has arrived." Her coaching model was "to set them up with tools so they are successful." She jumped in to guide the kitchen staff on how to handle multiple simultaneous orders by having them review the slips and prioritize the customer out front over any phone orders. She also helped make the sandwiches and other food to fill the orders. She cross-trained staff so they understood how to do various jobs without relying on notes tacked to the wall. She also directly addressed mistakes or customer service that fell below her high standards. When something went wrong, she asked, "So what are you learning from this?" After the staff answered, she reinforced their insights ("Exactly!") and then helped them find a solution. Her coaching focused heavily on customer service. She insisted that staff greet customers as they entered the café and pay more attention to customers in front of them than those calling in phone orders. She explained that customers in line might have wanted the last of an item in the case and would be upset if while they stood there it was sold to a phone caller. Employees began quoting to her and each other, "What would Linda do?" when they faced a dilemma. The owners believed some of the staff were relieved – especially those who opened up the business on their own in the early mornings.

Most of the changes Linda wanted were underway, and nearly all of the staff were onboard with her new ways of working and interacting with customers and each other. However, one afternoon as Linda kneaded the dough for the pastries to be baked for the display case, her watchful eyes followed a distressing interaction at the service counter. Emily waited on a customer who tried to order the previous day's special sandwich. Rather than check with the kitchen to ask if that was possible, or pitching the specials for that day, Emily told him emphatically that it wasn't possible to order yesterday's special. She waited silently while he reviewed the other menu items. Linda noted the customer's expression seemed displeased, and so was she. Linda had not fired any legacy employees as most had adopted her customer service approach over the several weeks since she took over. George's view was that if Emily had neither adapted nor been adding value, she needed to be replaced rather than them wasting time figuring out if she could be coached. Linda had to decide how to handle Emily.

Reflection Questions

1. Describe a time when you had a new supervisor or manager who made changes. What types of changes were easy for you and your coworkers to adapt to and which, if any, were a struggle?
2. If you have been in a leadership role, describe your approach to leading others. Give examples of when this style worked well for you, and situations where it might not have been as effective. If you are unsure about your style, ask a peer for feedback or take an online assessment (e.g., mindtools.com; verywellmind. com). If you haven't been in a leadership role, review descriptions of several leadership approaches and take an online assessment to learn what your

preferred style might be. Discuss situations in which you would be comfortable using this style and situations that might be more challenging.

Learning Applications

1. Analyze this situation using two course concepts, frameworks, or models so as to offer insights into what happened.
2. Research best practices for shaping or changing an existing organizational culture. What recommendations are best aligned with this situation and likely to have some effect?

Supplemental Readings

Fast Company. (July 31, 2002). 18 ways to take charge fast. Accessed at www.fastcompany.com/65159/18-ways-take-charge-fast

Peterson, S. J., Abramson, R., & Stutman, R. K. (2020). How to develop your leadership style: Concrete advice for a squishy challenge. *Harvard Business Review*, November–December, 1–11. Accessed at: https://hbr.org/2020/11/how-to-develop-your-leadership-style

Case 3   Reveal a Mistake to the Boss?

Trust and Psychological Safety in a Market Research Team

Amanda S. Patel

Synopsis

This case reveals a data science team lead's need to deal with an employee's error. The data science team was composed of three individuals who had collaborative, supportive relationships with one another, and mistakes were rare. They were part of the research division at a global market research firm. The data science team did not work with clients, but instead wrote code that client-facing teams utilized. In this case, one of the data scientists, Sean, made a mistake in his code which was then used by a client-focused team to create reports and presentations to an important client that the company had hoped would lead to additional clients in the future. When the data scientist realized his mistake, he reached out to his team lead, Chirag.

An Urgent Meeting: Setting the Stage

Chirag was Sean's team lead, and they were in the midst of a one-on-one meeting requested by Sean immediately after he learned he had made a coding mistake. During the meeting, Chirag could see that Sean was visibly upset. Chirag recognized that the mistake Sean made resulted in inaccurate data presentations to an important client. However, he expressed empathy and commented that Sean is human, and errors happen. As the meeting progressed, the two discussed the severity of the implications of the mistake and created a plan for assessing the extent of the damage.

GLB's Data Science Team

GLB Exploration Group was a global market research company that provided industry and firm-level data to clients about their consumers' attitudes, including customer satisfaction. Their products included research reports and client consulting. GLB employed thousands of people around the world in various divisions, one of which was the research division. Within the research division existed a data science team whose job was not to work directly with clients but to write code and analyze data that was then shared with others within GLB. A separate client-focused analyst team relied on that code to create presentations and share information with clients. Chirag Shah led the data science team. The geographically dispersed team consisted of himself, a data scientist level 3, Sean Price, a data scientist level 2, and Caitlin Blackshear,

DOI: 10.4324/9781003326298-7

a data scientist level 1. Chirag had been with the company for approximately three years and took over as the data science team lead approximately six months ago. Sean had also been with the company for over three years, and he had always been extremely dedicated and performed his job well. He received an "exceeds expectations" rating on his performance evaluation the prior year and was promoted from Level 1 to Level 2 data scientist at that time. Caitlin was the newest member of the team, having only been with the company for approximately one year.

The data science team was flexible and had the freedom to work whenever and wherever was best for their personal lives. As Caitlin described, "As a whole, you're pretty autonomous. You work at your own pace and are able to explore what you're doing on your own time and in your own environment." She also noted, "It is relatively high paced, constantly updating and learning. It is an environment where people are always learning."

They were also quite focused. Chirag, Sean, and Caitlin formed a close-knit team that met regularly, both on a schedule and spontaneously. In these meetings, they shared and bounced around ideas about how to do their work. The team felt comfortable asking one another questions about things that had stumped them. Caitlin commented, "It's collaborative, yet independent. We're all constantly bouncing ideas off each other or keeping each other in check. We could even be on the phone for 30 minutes just watching each other code. We're a trusting team. If we need each other's help, we're not afraid to reach out." They supported one another, even when the ideas weren't the best. Caitlin explained, "Within the data science team, it's like 'Hey, here's a better approach.' Nobody says you're wrong unless they have a solution. My team is very good in general." To illustrate, Sean mentioned an instance with Caitlin when there was a small process issue with data for an internal report. He noted that he "just mentioned briefly like 'Hey, this is something you can do a little bit better in terms of making the data legible for the person receiving it.'"

On an interpersonal level, as team lead, Chirag had built a strong relationship and excellent rapport with Sean and Caitlin. In describing Chirag's interpersonal behaviors, Sean and Caitlin described him as showing his support as a supervisor in the following ways:

- He "takes an interest in how we're feeling."
- He "always has open communication."
- He is "extremely supportive."

Furthermore, Chirag made it his goal to help Sean and Caitlin grow and develop professionally. As a result, he assigned them challenging tasks but provided support when they needed it. For example, if Sean struggled to get some aspect of his code to run properly, he did not hesitate to hop on a call with Chirag to discuss. The two then walked through the code together to solve the problem. To illustrate this aspect of the team, Sean stated, "On my immediate team, I've had lots of support and guidance and mentorship which is good."

A Mistake Was Made

Recently, members of the client-focused analyst team were working with some client data prepared from code written by Sean. For this dataset, Sean created code to combine smaller segments in the data and he named the variables so that they represented information from different, larger market segments for the client. This client, a health insurance company, was particularly important as others in GLB Exploration Group were hoping the health insurance company would be a champion for them and would advocate to other health insurance companies to also use GLB's services.

However, as the analysts were working with the data, they noticed that the numbers didn't add up in some of the larger segments, including self-insured, state-insured, and employer-insured. They mentioned the issue to Sean who immediately investigated the issue. Sean realized he made an error in the code. He had accidentally combined some of the employer-insured groups with some of the state-insured groups. Thus, the resulting data presented for both of those groups was a mix of state-insured and employer-insured groups.

Back to the Urgent Meeting: Managing the Aftermath

Unfortunately, reports and presentations had already been made for the client using this data. As a result, the analysts reported the wrong information to the client with regards to the state-insured and employer-insured market segments. Upon realizing his mistake, Sean immediately scheduled a meeting with Chirag. Sean explained, "When there is a data quality issue, the most important thing is to plug the hole as quickly as possible. My meeting with Chirag was to bring it to his attention and to get his opinion as to how it should be handled in terms of client communication and what work needed to be done." Chirag knew that in the meeting it was going to be important for him to be thoughtful in his response to the mistake. He also wanted to respond to Sean's feelings. Additionally, he needed to decide what to do next with regard to the potential for future mistakes by his team.

Reflection Questions

1. Consider a time when you or a colleague made a mistake at work. How did the manager react to the mistake? How did reactions to the mistake affect you or your colleagues?
2. Think about a job or volunteer position you've held. In what ways did managers or the organization encourage learning from failure? What, if anything, prevents learning from failure in that organization?

Learning Applications

1. Conduct an information interview with a manager. Ask how workplace mistakes made by employees have been handled in the past. What evidence is there at the company that employees are or are not comfortable revealing mistakes to managers?
2. Consider one of your current or past jobs, teams, or volunteer positions. Did it feel safe to reveal mistakes, errors, or a lack of knowledge in those settings, and why? Research best practices for creating psychological safety. Deepen your analysis of the psychological safety in those settings by identifying several practices that were used and some that were not.

Supplemental Readings and Video

Brassey, J., DeSmet, A., & Kruyt, M. (2023). 4 ways leaders can build "psychological safety" in their work teams. Accessed at: www.shrm.org/executive/resources/articles/pages/leaders-build-psychological-safety-teams.aspx

Edmonson, A. (2011). Learn from failure. Accessed at: https://hbr.org/video/2226539841001/learn-from-failure

Newman, L. C. (2023). The key to high-performing teams: Psychological safety. Accessed at https://thedecisionlab.com/insights/hr/the-key-to-high-performing-teams-psychological-safety

Case 4 The Outspoken Contractor
Inclusion and Conflict across Organizational Boundaries

Gina Vega

Synopsis

A manager who oversaw a large number of contract employees faced another instance of the ongoing conflict between them and the full-time workers in the facilities department where he worked. The manager must consider the sources of this conflict and the possible actions that could be taken to avoid similar problems in the future.

Another Clash

Peter Colonna, manager of contract employees at Seemore Systems, rubbed his face in frustration as he tried to decide how to deal with the latest contract employee crisis. About 40 percent of SeeMore Systems' technical workers were contract employees, hired from the Faria Facilities Agency, which had a positive long-term relationship with Seemore Systems.

The people hired from Faria Facilities Agency required some special handling due to the temporary nature of each employee's contract. For Peter, the constant onboarding of the contract workers to ensure they knew the basics of how to function at Seemore Systems (the company's structure, who to go to for different issues or questions, the organizational culture) was wearing. More challenging was when some of the contractors seemed to forget that full-time employees had significantly higher status in the organization than what was afforded to short-term contractors. Balancing the relationships between the two groups added considerable stress to Peter's job.

This time, the problem itself was simple. Fred Theiss, a contract project manager who worked for Faria Facilities Agency, had nearly come to blows with Carl Peruggi, the full-time manager of Seemore Systems' facilities department. They had disagreed over the assignment of particular employees to their two teams. Fred had been under the impression that he had a dedicated team for the project he had been brought in to complete for Seemore Systems. Carl believed that the employees in question were his resources to assign as needed, and he reassigned someone from Fred's team to another project. During the interaction, Fred interpreted Carl's brusque manner and assumption of privilege as abusive. Fred confronted Carl in the office bullpen and demanded an explanation for the reassignment of part of his team. The discussion, which began quietly enough, soon escalated into raised voices and finger pointing.

DOI: 10.4324/9781003326298-8

"You have to learn the way we do things here," cautioned Carl. "The people in this group report to the facilities department as a whole. That means they all report to me, not to you or any other contracted project manager." Fred's immediate and heated response was, "I don't have to learn … it seems that the way you do things is to berate people in front of others and badmouth an entire group of people without knowing what you're talking about."

Other workers couldn't avoid noticing the shouting match, but no one knew how to stop it. Finally, one of the other contractors picked up the phone and called Peter out of his meeting to attend to the fracas in the outer office. It took a couple of attempts at intervening with statements such as, "Whoa – what's going on here?" and "Let's quiet down and talk about this in my office," before the two men could be pacified enough to get them into Peter's office. They remained behind closed doors for more than an hour.

Shortly thereafter, the Faria Facilities Agency sent over its representative, Joanne O'Brien, to continue the discussion with Peter and senior management. They disappeared into Peter's office and called Fred and Carl in one at a time. The rest of the employees did not complete much work for the remainder of the day as they imagined what the final outcome of the public disagreement would be. The decision would likely have a lasting impact on their workload and their working relationships.

Reflection Questions

1. Think about an organization where you work or volunteer (or did so in the past). Were there groups of employees who had different levels of status? Explain why that may have been the case.
2. Think about a time when you or a colleague were involved in a conflict at work. What caused it and how was it resolved?

Learning Applications

1. Analyze this situation using two course concepts, frameworks, or models.
2. Talk with someone who is a manager. Ask about the different groups of employees at their organization to understand if some have preferred status over others. Explain why that may have been the case or what the organization does to prevent such differences from emerging. How do the differences (or lack thereof) affect interactions among employees?

Supplemental Readings

Concannon, M. (2020). Bridging the gap between contract staffing and company culture – How to make it work. Accessed at: www.linkedin.com/pulse/bridging-gap-between-contract-staffing-company-how-make-concannon/

Moore, A. (2018). How to manage conflict when working with third party contractors. Accessed January 13, 2024 at: www.contractorcompliance.io/post/how-to-manage-conflict-when-working-with-third-party-contractors

Part II

Navigating Power Relationships

Part II Introduction

Part II offers three cases that explore the power dynamics between managers and others in the organization. In Case 5 a young company co-founder used power in a way that jeopardized an inclusive climate as well as his employees' voice. In Case 6 a young manager was challenged by an older subordinate who did not comply with her requests. The case sits at the intersection of age, gender, and cultural norms around a leader's influence. In Case 7 the dynamic was reversed and a leader tried to curtail the offensive and discriminatory behaviors his own boss engaged in with others in the organization. The questions and readings below build on these themes of power, authority, leadership, coaching, and employee voice.

Part II Cases

Case 5, "Employee Voice at Bitfrost: Different Perspectives of Managers and Employees to Voice Behavior," is from the perspective of Mason Miller, 19, CEO and Co-founder of Bitfrost, a gaming studio focused on creating Roblox experiences for millions of players worldwide. Bitfrost's product became the largest third-party Roblox launcher in the world. In early 2021, the company's success was at risk when Bitfrost found itself in a time crunch to adjust to significant technological challenges posed by incompatibility with Roblox's latest update simultaneously with Apple's latest MacBook release. With only a few weeks to fix those issues, Bitfrost's software engineers blamed the situation on Mason and the management team. The software engineers set up a private meeting with each other, explicitly excluding the owners, to devise a solution. Mason had not approved of a meeting without him or his partners being present and reacted angrily to the developers' initiative. Readers wrestle with issues of employee voice and power dynamics with a young manager.

The learning objectives for this case include:

- Identify how employee voice and silence can bring change to an organization and work process.
- Examine how managers may react to employees claiming power in an organization.
- Compare different perspectives of managers and employees to voice behavior.

Case 6, "The Undermined Manager: Diversity, Influence Tactics, or Inexperience?" follows the situation of Katie Zeng, a 30-something year old administration manager of the

DOI: 10.4324/9781003326298-9

Asian Recreation Center (ARC). The population the ARC served was mainly first-genera-tion immigrants from East Asia who were at mostly in their mid-60s or older. Katie and her colleague Christine Ng were the only full-time employees and together were responsible for daily operations. Katie had to rely on part-time employees and volunteers to help run various events and programs held at the ARC. Those part-time employees and volunteers were either retired or in their second career, and recruited through referral. Katie found managing them challenging and wanted to know what she could do better, especially as her boss had a very different style. Katie's challenges around power and influence also involved managing up and navigating Asian cultural expectations.

The learning objectives for this case include:

- Students will diagnose how diversity affects workplace interactions.
- Students will analyze the sources of power and influence in a managerial interaction.
- Students will analyze the effect of different influence tactics a manager can use.

Case 7, "The Chairman's Jokes: Dealing with a Leader's Inappropriate Behavior," deals with a situation of workplace behavior in a French company from the point of view of the newly hired General Manager of US operations. His immediate supervisor, the Chairman of the Board, displayed inappropriate behavior, such as telling offensive jokes with sexual, racist and discriminatory content in business and social settings. The behavior was known to the human resources department to be against company policy. The situation touches on legal, management, and human resources perspec-tives and parallels the recent #MeToo Movement.

The learning objectives for this case include:

- Identify scenarios that may lead a business to accept behavior that is against its policies or potentially illegal in a business environment.
- Apply the basic principles of a corporate anti-discrimination and anti-harassment policy to an actual business scenario.
- Develop a listing of specific behaviors that may be considered harassing or dis-criminatory in business and personal settings.

Part II Supplemental Questions

Reflection Questions

1. Recall a situation at a job, volunteer position, sports organization, or other group to which you belonged that highlighted a clear difference in power between two or more people. What made the situation stand out to you (and others) and how did it relate to differences in power or influence?
2. Think of a situation when you wanted to challenge your manager or supervisor about something. Describe the situation and your decision to act or not. What factors did you weigh in making that decision?

Discussion Questions

1. How might a new manager establish authority without alienating subordinates?
2. How does an organization's culture influence the ways in which leaders use power?

3.   What are the challenges in managing individuals who are friends? What tactics might help the manager exert authority yet maintain positive relationships?
4.   How could subordinates influence a manager who behaves in unacceptable ways in the workplace? What options do they have to exercise power or influence their manager?

Part II Related Readings

Young Managers

Flesner, P. (2023). 7 steps to effective peer leadership. Accessed at: www.inc.com/patrick-flesner/7-steps-to-effective-peer-leadership.html

Horovitz, B. (2023). How to train young managers to supervise older employees. Accessed at: www.shrm.org/topics-tools/news/organizational-employee-development/how-to-train-young-managers-to-supervise-older-employees

Kurter, H. L. (2020). 4 ways you can build influence and succeed as a new manager. Accessed at: www.forbes.com/sites/heidilynnekurter/2020/08/28/4-ways-you-can-build-influence-and-succeed-as-a-new-manager/?sh=626a14915f30

Employee Voice in the Workplace

Burris, E. R. (2012). The risks and rewards of speaking up: Managerial responses to employee voice. Academy of Management Journal, 55(4), 851–875.

Mohammad, S. S., Nazir, N. A., & Mufti, S. (2023). Employee voice: A systematic literature review. Accessed at: https://doi.org/10.1177/23197145231153926

Young, J. (2024). Employee voice factsheet. Accessed at: www.cipd.org/en/knowledge/factsheets/voice-factsheet/

Managing Problematic Leaders

Crawshaw, L. (2010). Coaching abrasive leaders: Using action research to reduce suffering and increase productivity in organizations. *The International Journal of Coaching in Organizations*, 8(1), 60–77. Accessed at: www.bosswhispering.com/Coaching%20Abrasive%20Leaders.pdf

Gossard, B. (2018). Coaching up – How to give feedback to your boss. Accessed at: https://blakegossard.medium.com/coaching-up-how-to-give-feedback-to-your-boss-922b0f466f55

Kets de Vries, M. F. (2014). Coaching the toxic leader. *Harvard Business Review*, 92(4), 100–109.

Case 5   Employee Voice at Bitfrost

Different Perspectives of Managers and Employees to Voice Behavior

Matheus Fonseca

Synopsis

Mason Miller, 19, was the CEO and co-founder of Bitfrost, a gaming studio focused on creating Roblox experiences for millions of players worldwide. Bitfrost's product, Ardent Client, became the largest third-party Roblox launcher in the world. The company's success was at risk when Bitfrost found itself in a time crunch to adjust to significant technological challenges posed by incompatibility with the latest update of Apple's MacBook. With only a few weeks to fix these issues, software engineers blamed the situation on Mason and the management team. The software engineers set up a private meeting with each other, explicitly excluding the owners, to devise a solution. Mason had not approved of a meeting without him or his partners being present and reacted angrily to the developers' initiative.

A Private Meeting

The clock read 12:41 a.m. and the date was July 13, 2021. Mason Miller, CEO of Bitfrost, was meeting with his two business partners, James and Cory. They spoke about the current state of the company and future plans. Suddenly, they all heard a simultaneous notification on their phones from Slack. Jonathan, a senior developer at Bitfrost had sent the following message using the company-wide announcements channel: "Hey @client-developers, we would like to have a developer-only meeting to discuss our product, Ardent Client, as a project going forward. We'd like to talk about ways we can improve the development process for ourselves so we can all enjoy the work we're doing more." A When2Meet link followed in a second message so the developers could find the best time to get together.

Mason asked his partners if Jonathan had spoken to them before posting his messages; they both said no. Mason was furious, and thoughts immediately flooded his head. "Who does Jonathan think he is? Why is this a developer-*only* meeting? How do they expect to discuss the future of the project without the owners present?"

Industry Overview

Bitfrost focused its business on Roblox, one of the most popular video game of all time. Individuals and companies could turn their passion for the game into a business

DOI: 10.4324/9781003326298-10

by creating an experience, a custom multiplayer game world. Anyone with technical expertise could create an experience, customize it, and monetize it to millions of Roblox players. This model was appealing to business owners because Microsoft, the owners of Roblox, did not have any ownership of experiences, so all the revenue and intellectual property belonged to the experience owner. Another way individuals could make money was by creating and monetizing a Roblox client. Clients were direct modifications to the Roblox game files and could customize the game in more ways than an experience. Bitfrost had both, but the company's client, Ardent Client, was what made the company successful.

When Bitfrost released Ardent Client, it had one competitor who dominated the market, Indium Client, which GMA owned. GMA was an Italian esports organizer and production company that produced video game competitions worldwide. The company was founded in November of 2000, and in 2022, it sold for $1 billion to a Saudi government-backed tech company. When Ardent Client was released, Indium Client was generating millions of dollars, had over ten developers, and maintained a user base twenty times the size of Ardent Client's. These metrics proved true for over one year.

Company Background

Bitfrost was a software development company that specialized in game development. It was founded in January 2019 by three friends and former co-workers: Mason Miller, James Davis, and Cory Hayes. They were young and inexperienced in running a business. Mason, the youngest, was 18 years old. After opening a Roblox experience in February 2019, Bitfrost launched its second product Ardent Client, a third-party downloadable launcher for the game Roblox. Bitfrost had two software developers who worked part-time for little pay on it as a passion project that generated little income.

The Summer and Autumn of 2019 were rough. The three partners weren't paid, and the staff team was demotivated to continue supporting the project. In two months, Bitfrost had lost half of its staff team. It wasn't until a major technological breakthrough in late 2019 that Ardent Client became available to a greater audience. COVID-19 surprised everyone and countries worldwide shut down. Governments ordered millions of people to stay home. Many businesses suffered from this, but Ardent Client experienced immense growth. Management capitalized on the fact that people were at home and expanded the company's development team and hired content creators to advertise Ardent Client on social media. By 2022, Ardent Client had over 100 contractors on payroll, over two million monthly users, and had generated over $10 million in revenue.

Company Culture

Bitfrost's employees worked closely together, management promoted open dialogue and provided feedback, and after the work-day ended, they watched movies and played games. It was a digital company with no physical offices. Bitfrost employees and owners communicated in Slack, a messaging app, and Teamspeak, a voice communication app that was created to ensure all employees could join any channel they wanted, as long as there was not an active meeting. This allowed employees to collaborate on projects, exchange ideas, and build relationships. Whenever the owners worked on a new project or enacted any significant change, senior employees were given an opportunity to voice their opinions. All employees were notified about changes prior to them occurring to ensure no one felt excluded. James ensured that the developers could speak to him directly if there were any issues. He said, "I always sat on calls with our developers and listened to them speak their hearts about how things should be done. Sometimes, I even adjusted the way I did things so they could benefit."

The company embraced a bottom-up management style to ensure staff members suggested ideas about upcoming goals and projects. Tyler, the company's first hire and a close friend of the owners, recalled that he was encouraged to give suggestions directly to the owners. He said, "Management always listened to my opinions, even if they sounded crazy. There were times where management thanked me for my idea, but it never got implemented or further explored. I'm not sure if it's because they didn't have time or didn't like the idea, but that has happened a few times."

Ultimately, final decisions were made by the owners although the developers had a say. Cory said, "I've done my best to ensure our developers were comfortable speaking their minds, even if I disagreed with them. Whenever there was a disagreement on a technical issue, I invited developers to present their arguments, often spending hours discussing options and deciding on the best one." This environment allowed the owners and employees to grow extremely close to one another. Mason believed they saw each other as friends working towards a common goal who forgot about the employee-boss relationship. Mason knew this caused problems when more senior employees were unable to draw the line between friendship and work. For example, Tyler did not always agree with the decisions made. This caused tension when management asked Tyler to complete simple tasks. He pushed back, causing unnecessary arguments. He knew he could push the boundaries more than others due to his relationship with the owners and the unlikelihood of being punished. James said, "There were times when Tyler and I got into fiery debates because he disagreed with my decision. At the end of the day, I made the final decisions regarding Ardent Client's development. I listened to the developers, but I must do what I believe is best for the product. Not everyone in the team gets an equal vote in decision-making. If they did, our development process would be slow, and we wouldn't come to solutions."

Success and Challenges

Bitfrost released a significant update for Ardent Client in January 2021, overtaking its competition, Indium Client. The growth continued into March when Ardent Client had over 100,000 concurrent players online for the first time. Bitfrost hired two more developers to work on the client, which brought them to seven software engineers. The staff constantly worked on new updates and seemed to enjoy what they were working on. There was a lot of pressure from the player base to release continuous updates, and the team delivered. By April 2022, Bitfrost generated over $1 million in revenue. Ardent Client had gone viral on TikTok and Twitter, which increased advertising and media recognition.

Just as everything trended in the right direction, Bitfrost faced three unexpected technology challenges – each had the potential to seriously damage the company. A downside of Bitfrost's business was that it relied entirely on the game Roblox. If the owners of Roblox decided to shut down the game, Bitfrost would have instantly stopped generating income. Bitfrost also had to ensure its products were compatible with every update that Roblox released since players wanted to play on the latest version.

The first challenge was in April 2021, Roblox announced its newest update, version 1.17, which was set to release in early June. It was excellent news to players since all they had to do was press the "update" button. To game developers and companies like Bitfrost, the update required a complete overhaul of the codebase infrastructure, and Ardent Client's development team had only 2 months to prepare. Simply stated, Roblox migrated their infrastructure to a newer version. Ardent Client had to do the same, or else it would be unplayable on Roblox's latest versions. Roblox's developers also completely changed how the game was rendered on a player's computer screen. This required extensive work by Bitfrost's developers to ensure compatibility.

The second challenge occurred around that same time Apple released new MacBook computers that featured new M1 computer chips. The new chip was incompatible with Ardent Client. Since Mac players were 5–10% of Ardent Client, ensuring compatibility was a priority.

The third challenge was that Ardent Client was asked to remove one of its most popular features, Camera Mod. This new feature was added to Ardent Client so users could easily record their screen. Shortly after releasing it, Bitfrost learned from the mod's creator that they did not have the proper licenses to incorporate it. The license holders threatened Bitfrost with legal action, forcing them to completely remove this new feature.

Tension Increases as Challenges Intensify

During those challenging times, all developers worked on compatibility issues with MacBooks and Roblox. The team went from working on fun new projects and features to bug fixes, compatibility issues, and infrastructure overhauls. Morale decreased almost immediately when individual tasks were assigned. As collaboration on projects was at an all-time low, fewer team members interacted on Slack and Teamspeak. Some employees voiced concerns that they were highly frustrated and blamed the lack of new features and communication on the ownership team. One developer said "the reason we were fixing so many bugs and not adding features was because there was a lack of project management." The ownership team indicated issues had to be fixed to ensure Ardent Client succeeded and continued its growth trajectory and stated that it was unfortunate that all these issues arose simultaneously.

The clock was ticking, and time was of the essence. Ardent Client was nowhere close to supporting the Roblox update set to release on June 8, 2021. When it released, Ardent Client immediately lost tens of thousands of concurrent players. It wasn't until June 16 that a bare-minimum version of Ardent Client was compatible with Roblox's newest version. The M1 compatibility issues were not going to be fixed until July 2021. A summer that was meant to shatter records and achieve ambitious goals turned out to be one of Ardent Client's most challenging times.

The developers took matters into their own hands. Just after midnight on July 13th, Jonathan's Slack message about the private developers-only meeting went out to the entire company. This was the first time someone other than the owners posted a message in the announcements channel. This was also the first developer-only meeting without the owners present.

Mason initially believed that "Jonathan had spoken to Cory or James before posting. When I learned that he hadn't, I was extremely agitated. How could a developer who works for me think he could make these important decisions on his own? This sounded like a power grab, and I was not going to stand for it."

Mason was extremely angry and immediately asked Jonathan to join the call. Shortly after that Tyler joined. Mason felt disrespected. His authority as a founder and owner had been challenged for the first time. He yelled, asking who Jonathan thought he was and if he was out of his mind. "Tone it down a bit," James wrote in the owner's Telegram chat. "Yeah, don't be that mean," agreed Cory. "Screw that," replied Mason, as he continued to scream at Jonathan.

Mason told Jonathan he had no authority to set up a meeting excluding the owners without prior permission. After all, this was not Jonathan's team, it was Mason's. "How do you expect to talk about the future of my product without me being present?" asked Mason. After a few minutes of back and forth arguing, Jonathan attempted to de-escalate the situation by saying: "We just want to talk about what changes can be made in the management and work process that would make working here more enjoyable. We will not make any decisions without your approval. At the end of the day, this is my baby. I've put hundreds of hours into this project. I want to see it succeed. I would not do anything to negatively impact the team or project, and I apologize if my Slack message came off that way." At this point, Mason took a few deep breaths to calm down. The owners needed to decide if employees should meet without them, and what they really wanted when it came to employees speaking up at Bitfrost.

Reflection Questions

1. Think about a time when you or someone you know took the initiative at work or in a team only to discover the manager or others were unhappy about it. What was the cause of their pushback and how was it communicated? How did their reactions affect you or your colleagues?
2. What are the challenges of managing employees who are also friends?

Learning Applications

1. Research best practices for young managers and develop a list of strategies for fostering effective relationships with subordinates.
2. Conduct an information interview with a manager. What evidence is there that employees are willing to speak up with ideas or recommendations? What evidence is there that it is safe for employees to speak up or challenge the decisions or approaches of colleagues and managers?

Supplemental Readings and Podcast

Atkins, I. (2023). Characteristics of a good leader: Tips for new managers. Accessed at: www.businessnewsdaily.com/6456-new-manager-tips.html

LeaderFactor. (n.d.). Creating speak-up cultures at work. Accessed at: www.leaderfactor.com/learn/speak-up-culture-at-work

Clark, J. & Clark, T. (n.d.). Building a culture where employees feel free to speak up. Culture by Design podcast. Accessed at: www.leaderfactor.com/podcast/building-a-culture-where-employees-feel-free-to-speak-up

Zenger, J. & Folkman, J. (2015). What younger managers should know about how they're perceived. *Harvard Business Review*, September 29. Accessed at: https://hbr.org/2015/09/what-younger-managers-should-know-about-how-theyre-perceived

Case 6 The Undermined Manager

Diversity, Influence Tactics, or Inexperience?

Holly Chiu

Synopsis

Katie Zeng was in her early 30s and was the administration manager of an Asian Recreation Center (ARC). The population the ARC served was mainly first-generation immigrants from East Asia who were mostly in their mid-60s or older. Katie and her colleague Christine Ng were the only full-time employees and together were responsible for daily operations. Therefore, Katie had to rely on part-time employees and volunteers to help with various events and programs held at the ARC. Those part-time employees and volunteers were either retired or in their second career, and were recruited through referral. Katie found managing those people challenging and wanted to know what she could do better.

Another Incident

Katie Zeng was not happy to see all the receipts John Lin submitted. She remembered asking him to inform her before making any purchase. This was not the first time he had ignored her instructions, which made her really uncomfortable. She felt powerless and started to wonder what she should do next.

Asian Recreation Center

Katie Zeng has been the administration manager of an Asian Recreation Center (ARC) since 2017. The ARC was a non-profit organization in the northeast of the United States and had served local East Asian communities for four decades. ARC aimed to provide a venue for Asian immigrants to interact with each other and to facilitate interactions between Asian communities and local communities by hosting various cultural and language programs. The majority of the population the ARC served were first-generation immigrants who were in their mid-60s or older; therefore, the ARC also had a senior program especially designed for this age group. As members, they paid an annual fee which allowed them to participate in ARC's programs. The main sources of income of the ARC were donations and rental fees for their spaces such as the auditorium and meeting rooms used by other organizations for art and cultural activities. Donors' names were listed on the website as a way of showing appreciation.

DOI: 10.4324/9781003326298-11

The ARC was managed by a president, Jocelyn Wu, and a board of 20 directors. Katie and her colleague Christine Ng were the only full-time employees and together were responsible for daily operations. Christine was mainly responsible for external affairs, such as public relations, marketing, and community outreach. Katie was principally responsible for internal affairs, such as finances, managing art and cultural programs, and managing facilities. They worked independently but made all decisions together. They submitted a summary of ARC's activities to the president and board every two months unless there was something urgent or critical. In addition to Katie and Christine, there were two part-time employees, John Lin and Mary Kim, and volunteers recruited from time to time to facilitate the cultural and recreational programs held there.

Since ARC's mission was to be the gathering place for Asian immigrants, it held a number of regular programs during the week, such as language classes, karaoke classes, dance classes, etc. In addition to these regular programs, it also ran special events such as movie shows, holiday parties, and talks in the evening or on weekends. With so many programs running each week, and with only two full time employees, the ARC relied heavily on its volunteers and part-time employees, and Katie's responsibilities were to manage them. All part-time employees and volunteers were either retired or in their second career and were recruited through referral. They accepted the job because they either lived nearby or they had a lot of free time. Mary was in her mid-50s and came to the center once or twice per week. Her major responsibility was data entry and book-keeping. Even though John was a part-time employee, he was at the ARC every day. He was in his mid-60s and his job mainly involved keeping the offices clean, helping to set up for events, etc. Occasionally, he had to be at the ARC as early as 7 a.m. to prepare for the events and therefore he had keys to the facility. Katie could not hire more people due to budget constraints. She often relied on John for event set-ups. He was the only male among all the full-time and part-time employees, and Katie believed he was the strongest to move heavy things around.

Managing the Center

Katie was in her early 30s and had worked for the ARC for four years. She had a bachelor's degree in engineering and immigrated to the United States for a master's degree in business. After earning that, she applied for the job at the ARC and was hired by her predecessor. Katie worked part time when she was a student and had never held any managerial positions before this job. She was typically outspoken and direct and was not afraid of conflict. When she was in college she would not hesitate to argue if she deemed it necessary. After working for several years, she learned to pause and figure out what happened before engaging in a conflict. She believed that harmony and mutual respect were important in any relationship, and would say "We do not need to make another enemy." Since everything happening on the premises was her responsibility, her goal as manager of the ARC was to make it a welcoming place for everyone. Whenever there were disagreements of opinion at the ARC, whether they were between members or between a member and an instructor, she always invited everyone involved to have an open dialogue and listen to each other's perspectives. She hoped that everyone could take a step back and be considerate after understanding each other's point of view.

However, her approach did not work all the time. When she could not handle a situation, she would advise those involved to talk to Jocelyn, who took a very different approach. Jocelyn preferred to talk to each individual separately and persuade them to reach an agreement during those private conversations. Katie viewed this approach as being more concerned about making everyone happy than figuring out who was right and who was wrong. For example, a few times Katie found John using the auditorium and hanging out with friends without making a reservation or paying the rental fee. When she confronted him, he simply said he forgot to do it. Katie eventually reported this to Jocelyn, who said she would talk to him. Jocelyn's approach seemed to have worked, because after that, John did not use the auditorium without reservations. However, Katie also noticed that John was excused from paying for the previous uses. For Katie, rules were more important than personal relationships when managing a workplace. Katie believed that Jocelyn's way of handling such incidents undermined Katie's ability to exercise her authority for future violations.

Another day Katie was in the office when she heard noise from the auditorium. It was a quarrel between a student of the music program and an instructor of the dance program. She invited both to her office and tried to figure out a way to resolve the quarrel. The dance class instructor did not end the class in time because he wanted to finish playing the music, which meant the class overran by roughly two minutes. A student of the following music class just entered the auditorium and set up a karaoke machine when it was the class start time. The dance instructor felt this was dis- respectful and was irritated by it. However, the music student knew if his class did not start on time, he would have less time for his class. It was not a complicated situation, but the music student happened to be the husband of the manager of ARC's senior program. Therefore, when Katie asked Jocelyn to resolve the conflict, she preferred not to get involved and remained silent. Katie felt powerless again. She eventually put up a sign on the public bulletin board reminding all members using the space to be aware of the time, but she was still not sure those rules would be followed completely.

Taking Initiative or Challenging Authority?

After that incident there was a request for an evening table tennis program from members, because they wanted to play after work. To meet this need, the ARC had to have someone on site after the regular hours. Since John was at the ARC so much and he lived nearby, he agreed to oversee the evening table tennis program and do the cleanup afterwards. To facilitate this he purchased tables, balls, and rackets. However, he did not get approval from Katie before making the purchases, which upset her. The normal procurement process at the ARC was for the person to make a list of items needed and send the list to Katie for review. Katie would check the inventory to see if the purchases were required. It created a problem for Katie when John made a pur- chase without informing her in advance. When Katie confronted him, he replied "I need the equipment for the program. Why do I need your approval? Who do you think you are?" Katie paused when she heard those comments.

Katie liked her job but she felt exhausted as well. She felt no one really listened to her because they believed she was too young and inexperienced to solve their pro- blems. Even though she had taken graduate management courses, she still found it a challenging situation. She really wanted some advice on how to make her work life easier.

Reflection Questions

1. For various reasons, some employees in organizations are given more leeway to "bend the rules." Describe a time when you (or someone you know) worked or volunteered somewhere and received special benefits, perks, or the freedom to not follow the rules exactly. What were some of the benefits and disadvantages in that situation?
2. Consider a time when a manager, leader, or team member you worked with was from a different ethnic background or age group. What synergies or challenges did you experience?

Learning Applications

1. Analyze the situation using two course concepts, frameworks, or models so as to offer insights into what happened.
2. Consider the situation from President Wu's perspective and propose three actions she might take to improve Katie's situation. Indicate whom the action is targeting, and how it will create change.

Supplemental Readings

Hill, L. A. (2007). Becoming the boss. *Harvard Business Review*, 85(1): 48–57.

Indeed Editorial Team. (2022). Power in leadership: 9 types for effective leaders. Accessed on June 2, 2023 at: www.indeed.com/career-advice/career-development/typ es-of-power-in-leadership

Yang, L. (2019). 7 ways I've learned to assert myself as a young woman at work. Accessed on June 2, 2023 at: www.fastcompany.com/90416521/7-ways-ive-learned-to-assert-myself-as-a-young-woman-at-work

Case 7   The Chairman's Jokes

Dealing with a Leader's Inappropriate Behavior

Ralf Mehnert-Meland

Synopsis

Thomas recently joined a French company as general manager of its US operations. His immediate supervisor, the chairman of the board, displayed inappropriate behavior, such as telling offensive jokes with sexual, racist, and discriminatory content in business and social settings. The behavior was known to the HR department and against company policy.

A Global Business Assignment

Thomas Claes was a seasoned business executive. He had moved from his native Belgium to the United States to pursue his education in business and management. For the past 20 years, Thomas had worked in business development and management positions in the United States for French and US steel manufacturing companies. While he had grown up in Belgium and had a Belgian-American cultural identity, his business identity was firmly rooted in the business and human resource principles practiced in the United States. He had been trained in several large US companies on how to identify and address issues such as harassment and discrimination.

He also was a strong advocate of equal rights in his personal life. Thomas and his partner were active in several professional and social organizations advocating minority and LGBTQ+ causes. While his interest and participation were known, he did not actively advertise them in his work environment.

Thomas had recently joined the US subsidiary of a French specialty steel manufacturing company in an executive position at its headquarters near San Francisco, California. After a few months in his new role, his supervisor, the general manager of the subsidiary, abruptly resigned. François Dubois, the chairman of the board of the entire company, personally asked Thomas to be the new general manager to quickly fill the void left by the departure. Thomas agreed and was promoted. He was the third manager of the company's US operations in fewer than six months. In his new role, he directly reported to François. He also received a substantial salary increase.

François was the highly energetic and very engaging leader of the company. He was fun-loving and liked to party. Company social events were known as epic productions with bands, good food and alcohol. Business dinners with François were

DOI: 10.4324/9781003326298-12

equally entertaining and luxurious. The official events and dinners were often followed by after-hour activities in various bars that lasted into the early morning hours.

Unfortunately, François also had a less charming side. He was prone to making very spontaneous business and personnel decisions, triggered often by side discussions during the after-hour activities. His enthusiasm and top position within the company's hierarchy made it very difficult to challenge his decisions or provide alternative solutions. He sometimes displayed very forceful behavior and would demand immediate implementation of his ad hoc decisions. François's behavior was generally known by the employees. There often were subtle comments made about him. "Did you hear what happened at …" was a common opening line when employees would discuss François's behavior at a recent meeting, dinner or social event. As a result of his position and overall very engaging character, however, the employees tended to accept the more negative aspects as part of the "overall package."

Thomas's Challenge

Thomas enjoyed his new elevated position and responsibilities. The company was growing, profitable and in an exciting industry. It was still privately owned but had plans to become a publicly traded company and raise significant funds for a large global expansion. The US subsidiary included several offices around the country. While the US team had gone through difficult times because of the recent multiple changes in their leadership and needed rebuilding, Thomas believed that the team would be very successful going forward. He was especially excited about its great diversity, including team members from twelve different countries, different racial backgrounds and several openly gay employees.

During Thomas's first month in his new position, the company received a letter from his predecessor's personal attorney. The former general manager claimed that the company had created a hostile work environment by not addressing explicit sexually charged jokes made by François in multiple instances. In addition, Thomas began noticing a strange pattern of behavior developing when he was with François either in one-on-one or group situations: François was very fond of making disparaging remarks about others based on their looks, gender, skin color and other attributes. He also liked to make jokes. Many of the remarks and jokes had blatantly offensive and often very graphic racial, sexual or anti-gay connotations or were outright aimed against women, non-whites or gay individuals.

Thomas did not agree with these statements. He told the chairman a number of times in private that such comments were inappropriate, could be misread and might negatively impact the cohesion of the team. He also pointed out that the rules and cultural expectations in the US were much stricter regarding these matters than those in France. François would brush off those suggestions with statements like: "This is all in fun. And it is OK to say as long as no one in the audience is part of group that I am making fun of." Despite Thomas's insistence that the statement was not true, the chairman continued to make the offensive jokes in meetings with company employees, as well as meetings with representatives from other companies, customers and potential customers.

Company Policies in Place

The company had in place very clear personnel policies against harassment and discrimination that applied to all its employees worldwide. The policies were enforced by the global and local human resources departments. The company's employee handbook included the following language and every employee agreed to abide by it as part of their employment contract with the company:

> All Team Members must always conduct themselves in a business-like manner while on our Company's property or while conducting business for our Company. All Team Members must treat fellow Team Members, customers, partners and visitors to our Company with dignity and respect.
>
> Our Company is committed to providing a work environment free of sexual harassment and harassment or discrimination based on race, color, national origin, gender, religion, age, disability or any other protected characteristic established by Federal or State laws. Our Company prohibits all behavior that constitutes or could lead or contribute to harassment and discrimination.
>
> Requests for sexual acts, unwelcome sexual advances, touching, remarks or other conduct of a sexual nature are prohibited, as are any discriminatory acts or remarks. Any substantiated incidents of sexual harassment, harassment or discrimination by another Team Member will result in immediate disciplinary action up to and including termination.
>
> This policy applies to all Team Members.

Having had no success changing the chairman's behavior, Thomas made a confidential call to Ines Kellermann, the company's global head of human resources, to discuss the situation and possible avenues to address it. To his surprise, Thomas found that the issue was well-known by the HR department and that several (unsuccessful) attempts had been made to try and change the chairman's offensive behavior. There actually was a concern in the HR department that the company was subject to legal exposure in the United States because of its much stricter harassment and discrimination laws and regulations. These stricter rules had been the reason the company had developed the very clear language in the employee handbook and applied it to all employees around the world – even those in locations with less strict rules, such as the headquarter location in France. Ines also was concerned about negative publicity as the #MeToo movement had just started to uncover instances of sexual harassment and assault in many industries around the world.

Ines and Thomas agreed to develop a short and confidential action plan to try and change the chairman's behavior, assess the attitude of the US employees and identify potential legal exposure. In view of the sensitivity of the issue, the two decided to execute the plan subtly and, when asked, pretend it was part of an overall refresher for the team of the company's policies. They also agreed to review the findings within two months and then determine next steps or necessary changes.

The main steps of the action plan were to be:

1. Thomas would talk to François in private and clearly spell out the potential legal exposure of the offensive comments and jokes for the company.
2. Ines would send an email to all employees to remind them – in a positive manner – of the company's policies regarding harassment and discrimination.
3. Thomas would talk to his directors who were directly reporting to him to stress the importance of those policies.

4. He would also have one-on-one meetings with each director to try to discover whether there were any direct concerns about François's behavior.

One More Incident

Before the two could finalize and start implementing the plan, another incident occurred. The chairman and the company's global chief technology officer visited the US operations as part of an executive tour of the company's main offices. The two, Thomas, and four of his directors had dinner in downtown San Francisco. After Thomas had left the group for the evening, the chairman made a number of offensive and graphical anti-gay comments. The new CTO joined in with several discriminatory statements and jokes regarding the gay population in San Francisco. The following day, one of the directors filed a formal complaint with the human resources department claiming that the company was creating a hostile and discriminatory work environment. The director's uncle, who was also one of the company's outside financial consultants, was openly gay. The director felt the comments and jokes were highly offensive, inappropriate, and against company policy. Thomas instructed the HR department to immediately follow up and review the claim. The review found that the comments and jokes did not amount to an actionable claim and – while in poor taste – were not made with discriminatory intent. When asked why she made the comments, the global CTO stated that she did not think they were an issue because "François does this all the time." To Thomas's surprise, Ines decided not to pursue this matter any further even though the three other directors attending the dinner had stated in the review process that they considered the statements and jokes as offensive.

The Final Straw

Less than a week after the report, the chairman ordered Thomas to move the director to a less desirable position with the company, an action that was a de facto demotion. Thomas met François in person and forcefully told the chairman that the decision to demote the director was wrong. It also could be construed as illegal retaliation, and he would not support it. The chairman rejected his arguments and insisted on immediate demotion. Thomas also spelled out in very clear and direct language that the continuation of this offensive behavior could result in legal exposure for the company and that it already had a negative impact on Thomas's attempts to rebuild the US team. The chairman merely thanked Thomas for bringing up his concerns but did not see any reason to pursue them any further. He said the decision was final, that Thomas had no more say in it, and directed him to demote the director the next day.

Reflection Questions

1. Describe a time when you received feedback about your own behavior or attitudes that did not match your self-perception. What contributed to any resistance or openness to accept the feedback?
2. Describe offensive behavior in the workplace that you witnessed, heard about, or experienced. How did colleagues or managers handle the situation and what were the outcomes?

Learning Applications

1.   Analyze the situation using two course concepts, frameworks, or models so as to offer insights into what happened.
2.   Research current legal guidelines in your region or country regarding the definition of harassment and the responsibilities of managers and organizations.

Related Readings

Gallo, A. (2017). How to respond to an offensive comment at work. *Harvard Business Review*, February 8. Accessed at: https://hbr.org/2017/02/how-to-respond-to-an-offensive-comment-at-work

SHRM. (n.d.). Managing difficult employees and disruptive behaviors. Accessed July 7, 2023 at: www.shrm.org/resourcesandtools/tools-and-samples/toolkits/pages/managingdifficultemployeesa.aspx

Acknowledgement

This case was originally published by the author in the *International Journal of Instructional Cases* (2022) and was adapted to this volume with permission of the publisher.

Part III

Handling Workplace Conflict

Part III Introduction

Part III includes three cases that involve conflict in the workplace. In Case 8 a non-profit organization must deal with the sudden outburst and resignation of a board member following a decision to exclude her. In Case 9 the conflict is embedded in the responsibilities and coordination between two interdependent groups working for the same department. In Case 10 the conflict emerges between employees and customers, and then management is left to determine what happened, and importantly, how to prevent it from happening again. Together, these cases present very different situations that tap into a dynamic that many managers find uncomfortable to handle. The questions and readings below build on these themes of interpersonal conflict, stereotypes and biases as causes of conflict, and managing conflict in the workplace.

Part III Cases

Case 8, "Place of Hope and the Board Meeting Disruption," centers on conflict and volunteer management in a $1.8 million human service organization that offered nutrition and housing services in a low-income area. A Board meeting was disrupted when an unhappy Board member yelled at the Board Chair and other volunteer board members, and then resigned and left the meeting. The member was upset at not being invited to join a committee in their area of professional expertise. The Board Chair had tried and failed to reach the member. The episode occurred in front of a group of people who were deeply invested in the consequences of the meeting, which magnified possible negative consequences. The incident was markedly different from the Board culture of congeniality and the Chair wondered about his own role in the conflict. In the days after the meeting, the Chair evaluated the episode and considered what actions were needed to preserve the best elements of its Board governance and previously positive interactions, and how to move the group past the incident. The case provides opportunities to evaluate the sources and paths of conflict, its avoidance, and conflict communications as well as their impact on organizational processes in the particular setting of a nonprofit Board.

The learning objectives for this case include:

- Analyze and assess a conflict episode, including its precursors and possible steps that could have prevented or resolved the conflict.

DOI: 10.4324/9781003326298-13

- Assess how conflict within an episode is expressed, including the directness and intensity.
- Evaluate the potential effectiveness of a nonprofit's board governance processes.

Case 9, "Conflict Unveiled: Intergroup Blame Between Information Technology Teams," focuses on the conflict between two teams in the information technology (IT) department of a jewelry company (Parrl Inc.). The team leaders, Oscar Ramos and Jonathan Rogers, are at an impasse regarding which team is responsible for missing data. Their conflict and its impact on company operations caught the attention of senior leadership, who directed their manager to resolve the issue. This case allows students to diagnose conflict within the IT department, apply various management approaches to resolve it, and suggest solutions to resolve this inter-department conflict.

The learning objectives for this case include:

- Diagnose the type of conflict within Parrl Inc.'s IT department.
- Apply various methods of conflict management and select the most appropriate method.
- Implement the various steps of the selected conflict management approach and assign the appropriate roles to the various parties, including the senior manager in the IT department.

Case 10, "Bias or poor training? The Wine Train Incident," describes how members of the Sistahs on the Reading Edge Book Club were ejected from the Napa Valley Wine Train for noise, despite having made a reservation that indicated their need for seating assignments where they could be less quiet. Conductors warned them about noise prior to departure and again once while on the train before ejecting them with a police presence. This incident presents an opportunity to consider conflict management strategies used by service personnel. It also pushes readers to consider how stereotypical thinking may influence decision-making, and why managers must watch for potential biases in their operational processes.

The learning objectives for this case include:

- Identify and analyze the implications of the management and communication issues in play within the context of this conflict.
- Formulate possible antecedents and consequences of the concerns, perceptions, and behaviors portrayed.
- Determine the role of communication in the emergence and resolution of the situation presented.
- Critically examine the logical approaches a company employee might take in response to the situation and hypothesize possible outcomes resulting from the decisions made.

Part III Supplemental Questions

Reflection Questions

1. Describe an interpersonal conflict you were involved in at work, school, or in a team/group. Who was involved, what were the sources of the conflict, what was

your role in the situation, and how did you handle or respond to the conflict? Use concepts related to conflict management to identify the ideal approach to handling that situation and assess how well it was handled.

2.   Consider a time when you observed a conflict at work that appeared to be based on assumptions or stereotypes about an individual or group. What aspects of the situation made you believe it was motivated by bias? Assess how the situation might have been handled differently, and how the underlying causes of the conflict could have been addressed.

3.   What are your strengths and weaknesses when it comes to dealing with conflict in a professional setting? What has contributed to your skill and approach in handling conflict?

Discussion Questions

1.   The three cases in Part III all involve conflict in the workplace. What similarities and differences exist among the sources of those conflicts?
2.   Describe possible systems or methods that the organizations in the three cases could each introduce to prevent or minimize these types of conflicts in the future.
3.   Assess the role that communication might have played in the conflicts outlined in these cases.

Part III Related Readings

Managing Interpersonal Conflict

Angelica, M. P. (2002). Eight steps to managing conflict. *Nonprofit World*, 20(4) (July–August), 29–32. Accessed at: www.snpo.org/members/Articles/Volume20/Issue4/V200429.pdf

Hare, G. (2022). Managing interpersonal conflict in the workplace. Accessed at: https://hrconnect.com.au/blog/managing-interpersonal-conflict-in-the-workplace/

Mind Tools Content Team. (n.d.). Conflict resolution. Accessed at: www.mindtools.com/ahcpfn4/conflict-resolution.

The Conflict Resolution Network provides 12 podcasts focused on developing an understanding and skills around a win-win approach, the roles of empathy and creativity, managing emotions, cooperating, assertiveness, and more. It can be accessed at: www.crnhq.org/podcasts/.

Biases Related to Differences or Groups

Feldberg, A. C., & Kim, T. (2018). How companies can identify racial and gender bias in their customer service. *Harvard Business Review*, May. Accessed at: https://hbr.org/2018/05/how-companies-can-identify-racial-and-gender-bias-in-their-customer-service.

Holland, E. (2024). Intergroup conflict: Causes, consequences, and solutions. Accessed at: www.adrtimes.com/intergroup-conflict/

Nickerson, C. & McCleod, S. (2023). Intergroup conflict. Accessed at: www.simplypsychology.org/intergroup-conflict.html

Case 8   Place of Hope and the Board Meeting Disruption

Roland J. Kushner

Synopsis

Place of Hope was a $1.8 million human service organization in a low-income area of Hillside, a city in the Northeast, offering nutrition and housing services. A board meeting was disrupted when an unhappy board member yelled at the board chair and other volunteer board members, and then resigned and left the meeting. The member was upset at not being invited to join a committee in their area of professional expertise. The board chair had tried and failed to reach the member. The episode occurred in front of a group of people who were deeply invested in the consequences of the meeting, which magnified possible negative consequences. The incident was markedly different from the board culture of congeniality and the chair wondered about his own role in the conflict. In the days after the meeting, the chair evaluated the episode and considered what actions were needed to preserve the best elements of its board governance and previously positive interactions, and how to move the group past the incident.

Not a Dream

It was a beautiful spring day in Hillside when Joel, chair of the board of directors of Place of Hope (PoH), woke up. He felt happy to see the sun and feel the new season coming on … but then he thought about the difficult board meeting held the previous afternoon. While getting ready for board meetings was always hard work, they were usually productive. The last meeting had been unusual, and Joel felt less cheerful. He and other board members willingly took on volunteer governance roles at Place of Hope, a community nonprofit, even though it meant juggling that with their busy personal and work lives. He now needed the board to move beyond the disruption and address several governance issues related to PoH's recent growth and the need to implement their succession plan for the CEO's position.

Place of Hope

Place of Hope was a 30-year-old human services 501(c)(3) nonprofit with primary services in nutrition, housing, case management, and financial trusteeship. With about 15 full-time employees and several part-time staff, its programs included a meal center and food bank that served about 9,000 people per year, dozens of housing units including both

DOI: 10.4324/9781003326298-14

transitional and permanent housing as well as shelter, as well as counseling, and financial trusteeship. Despite the ongoing economic recovery from the Great Recession, persistent poverty in the northeastern city of Hillside and its region had expanded demand for services. The budget of $1.8 million was funded by local, state, and federal contracts, rental revenues, and high levels of community giving. PoH had broad private support from individual donors, prominent regional and some national companies, and foundations. The budget grew by 30% over the CEO's eight-year leadership as PoH added staff and programs. It was well-regarded for its impact on the populations and areas served, and for relationship-building, public relations, and communications activities. The CEO was viewed as a strong manager and a well-informed policy advocate who was often asked to join or advise regional networks addressing housing and hunger issues.

PoH's board of 15 volunteers had a mix of long-standing and newer members, including busy professionals in law, engineering, and education, mid- and senior-level business leaders, and retirees. While it was primarily White until the early 2010s, the board evolved to include more Latino and Black members, reflecting the Hillside community it served. Several board members had needed public assistance or services earlier in their lives; one had even used PoH's food bank to feed her young family. Collectively, the board had expertise in finance, real estate, law, and management, as well as non-profit sector skills in program design, volunteer management, resource development, and community relationships. Many members served on other community boards, but almost all volunteered for PoH with client or professional services, securing donations from their employers or networks, or giving from their own resources, some at substantial levels.

The bylaws made the chair responsible for assigning directors to serve on standing and *ad hoc* committees, which were established from time to time. Standing committees included bylaws, development (fundraising), finance, and nominations; the executive committee included the officers (chair, vice-chair, secretary, treasurer, assistant treasurer) and one at-large. The board regularly worked on governance processes: reviewed bylaws, formalized the nominations processes, conducted a self-assessment, codified expectations for participation and attendance, and broadened the range of experience of its members. While the Board culture was congenial and friendly, members were attentive to the strategic, financial, and oversight decisions. Meeting agendas were distributed days beforehand.

There were six scheduled board meetings each year, and the executive committee met on alternate months and as needed. Meetings were typically held in late afternoons at mid-week. The bylaws specified that regular attendance at board meetings was a duty, one that was honored for the most part. One exception was a member who rarely attended, but had previously led several successful fundraising events and had secured a large gift from his employer to PoH.

Joel was in his sixth year on the board, and second as chair. He knew that turnover in board membership in local nonprofits was normal because of life or career changes, as he welcomed new board members and said farewell to others every few months. In Joel's experience, no PoH board member had ever departed due to overt conflict over personality or policy, though some chose not to renew or had not been renominated because of problematic attendance.

Before the Board Meeting

After musing aloud for several years about retiring, the CEO informed Joel and the executive committee that she wanted to conclude her work by year's end. Joel also learned that Beatrice, another strong member, chose not to seek another three-year term as chair of the Nominations committee. She had been elected to lead the board of another community nonprofit, and though she loved PoH she was unable to give the attention it needed. Her departure left a vacancy in her current role, which sought and evaluated candidates for the board. These two changes required immediate shuffling of board member responsibilities to help in a CEO search, and to chair nominations.

Samantha was a likely person to be asked to assist with these tasks and lead the search. She was in her third year on the board, her second year on the nominations committee, and had been somewhat active in reviewing prior nominees. Professionally, she was a manager with responsibilities in one region for a multi-state company. Her employer made an annual donation to PoH that placed it in a lower tier of business supporters. Overall, she had been a relatively passive participant in board policy discussions and absent more than most members from both board and committee meetings. Samantha had been nominated to the board by Gavin, a professional who had worked at another firm with Samantha, and had thought well of her. However, he had expressed concern to the executive committee over her absences.

Nonetheless, Samantha had the expertise for a search and was the most likely person to lead the nominations committee next. Joel hoped to get her ideas about the search, and see if she was willing to join the search committee. Ten days before the meeting, Joel called and emailed several times asking Samantha to be in touch about PoH activity; he got no response. It was not the first time he had difficulty getting Samantha to return calls or set up a meeting. Over the next few days, he invited five other board members to join the search committee; after they all readily agreed, he stopped pursuing Samantha. Joel had mounting priorities at his day job and efforts to engage Samantha had taken up a lot of time. There was no indication that continued efforts would succeed. Everyone else had said yes, so he decided not to include Samantha in the search committee.

The Board Meeting

The board met at 4 p.m. on Tuesday in the conference room where one of the directors worked. The participants consisted of:

- Eleanor: CEO
- Beatrice: board member, nominations committee chair
- Charlotte: board member
- Gavin: board member, executive committee member
- Joel: board chair, executive committee member
- Samantha: board member, nominations committee member
- Seven other board members and two staff members
- One invited guest.

PoH periodically invited prospective board members to observe a meeting as part of the nominations process, and one guest was in attendance. The senior staff was present, as was customary. Three board members were absent. Samantha arrived after the meeting was underway, so Joel did not get to speak with her privately first. First, the CEO announced her retirement, though most knew of it. The agenda then addressed other significant governance issues: the bylaws review, a large upcoming real estate transaction, and a discussion of the implications of a funding shift for a major program. When the succession plan came up on the agenda, Joel announced the search calendar in coming months, and those members who had agreed to serve on the search committee.

Samantha, not hearing her name mentioned, appeared to be upset, and raised her voice to inquire why. Joel replied that Samantha had not responded to several invitations to talk and was frequently absent. She berated Joel for overlooking her knowledge, pointed at him and said "You suck!" She then pointed to Charlotte (one of the search committee) and said, "Who do you think you are? You're the one causing this." Samantha stood up, gathered her papers, announced she was resigning, and left the room, closing (not slamming) the door behind her. Charlotte, totally stunned, turned to the person in the next seat and said, "I have had only two interactions with this person and I perceived them to be very pleasant." The episode took less than 60 seconds.

After Samantha left, there was quiet. Everybody sat up straight, and most appeared surprised. Joel was shaken; his preparations had not included thinking about conflict. As people shifted in their seats, he spoke quietly and resumed the meeting. He stated that it was unfortunate, but he had nothing to add, and reiterated his attempts reach Samantha at a busy time. He suggested proceeding with the agenda. As he hoped, no one expressed a desire to discuss Samantha. The board resumed its path through the meeting agenda, though Joel thought some of the usual good energy was missing. The remaining agenda items were not contentious, but the level of engagement was low. When they adjourned around 6:30 p.m., there were brief and informal conversations before everyone headed home. Joel heard supportive comments ("Good job keeping your cool" was one), as well as surprise at Samantha's conduct. There was little chance to speak with the guest. Joel could not help feeling that it was a sad and embarrassing episode.

After the Board Meeting

Reflecting on the previous day's meeting and thinking about the future, Joel wanted to enjoy the pleasant weather, but he had damage control in mind. He hoped to minimize the negative impact on Place of Hope, maintain the board's collegiality, and move forward with governance activities and the search for a new executive director. Gavin (who initially nominated Samantha) emailed Joel asking him to forgive Samantha and readmit her to the board. Gavin wrote that it was his own initiative, and he was not acting on Samantha's request. Another board member emailed support for Joel's handling of the matter and his leadership communications in general. In conversation, Eleanor confirmed that Samantha was chronically difficult to reach, and advised against readmitting her. Joel felt no desire to do so, but was prepared to discuss it if she asked. However, Samantha was silent.

Joel was concerned about his own leadership practice. He didn't doubt Samantha had behaved unprofessionally, but had his own conduct provoked it? Had he been forthright about the reason for contacting Samantha, and/or extended Samantha enough courtesy? Conversely, he wondered how many times it was reasonable for one volunteer to ask another to respond to messages.

Samantha's departure, ironically, made it more urgent to recruit new board members. Fortunately, the prospects Beatrice, Eleanor, and Joel had recommended to the search committee seemed promising. As days slipped by, time demands from work and family continued, and the PoH board confronted other governance work. But the unhappy memory of the meeting disruption remained, and Joel wondered what else he and the board could do to maintain collegiality and progress.

Reflection Questions

1.   Put yourself in Joel's place. What are three ways that you could respond if you were running a meeting and someone had an outburst and said harsh words to you?
2.   Some nonprofits have policies that remove board members who miss a certain number of meetings. However, these policies may lead to uncomfortable conversations and are sometimes hard to enforce. What are the benefits and disadvantages of strictly following those policies when a board member is absent too much?

Learning Applications

1.   Analyze the situation using two course concepts, frameworks, or models so as to offer insights into what happened.
2.   Describe a time when you experienced or observed a similar unexpected outburst. What caused it and how was it handled?

Supplemental Readings

Hebert, J. (2019). Nonprofit arts boards play crucial (and complex) role. *The San Diego Union Tribune*, December 9. Accessed March 10, 2023 at: www.sandiegou niontribune.com/entertainment/theater/sd-et-theater-boards-20161128-story.html

Matthews, K. (2019). How to recognize and avoid volunteer burnout. Accessed at: https://blogs.volunteermatch.org/how-to-recognize-and-avoid-volunteer-burnout

McDonald, E. G. (2023). Managing board conflict. Accessed at: https://turningpoin tresolutions.com/managing-board-conflict/

Case 9   Conflict Unveiled

Intergroup Blame between Information Technology Teams

Ankur Nandedkar and Roger S. Brown

Synopsis

Within the information technology (IT) department of a jewelry company (Parrl Inc.), two teams led by Oscar Ramos and Jonathan Rogers were at an impasse regarding which team should be responsible for the missing data gathered in the Enterprise Data Warehouse. Their conflict and its impact on company operations caught the attention of senior leadership and their manager Kevin Behrendt had to fix the situation and ensure it would not happen again.

Missing Data

Kevin Behrendt, the senior IT manager of Parrl, Inc., a jewelry company with over $5 billion in revenue in 2018 and over 20,000 employees, was called into an emergency meeting to explain why the company's top management received an incomplete sales data report. Kevin was shocked since this was the first incomplete report in the last five years. Top management noticed the omission of information reflecting how often existing customers make purchases and how much they spent in person or online for each quarter. After an analysis, Kevin found multiple errors in the sales report due to missing customer data. The top management directed him to meet with the leads of the two teams that collected and managed the data and to return with a completed sales report in two weeks. Kevin agreed to fix it within the two weeks as specified, and he didn't let on that there was tension between the two teams.

Collaboration Between the IT Teams

The information technology (IT) division of Parrl Inc. Jewelry supported complex business operations for retail store sales, a strong virtual presence with online sales, inventory management, and sales tracking. The company invested significantly in business data analytics as a critical aspect of the company's strategic planning to further expand its business by better serving customers' needs, and experienced increased sales. The IT division was staffed by over 500 people and organized into several teams. It also supported other functional areas within the company, gathered customer data, maintained customer interface software, and provided technical support for customers. It played a significant role in managing business operations and enhancing revenue.

DOI: 10.4324/9781003326298-15

Kevin started as a programmer and moved up the ranks to become the senior IT manager for Paarl Inc, with over 20 years of experience in the IT industry. He previously served as the leader of both the Enterprise Data Warehousing (EDW) team and the Reporting team during his years in the IT division before being promoted to the senior IT manager position.

Ongoing IT projects were under his leadership, including a plan to re-engineer business processes by utilizing technology to improve efficiency and reduce overhead costs. Customer data analytics was an integral part of the project to revamp the customer relationship management (CRM) system and the real-time inventory management (IM) system. The CRM system gathered various aspects of customer information such as their name, age, total purchases, product interests, household income, etc. (referred to internally as the "360 degrees of information about a customer"). The CRM system was expected to generate more sales leads by providing customer information to the company's marketing and customer service divisions. The primary purpose of the IM system project was to ensure that as soon as a purchase was made, the inventory data was immediately updated to different teams (e.g., the merchandising division and sales staff). This real-time inventory information helped customers who visited the jewelry store website to go to the stores where the particular items were available. The staff directed customers who entered the store and might not have used the online real-time inventory information to other stores where the item of interest was available. Two teams in particular were instrumental in business analytics utilizing customer data: EDW and Reporting.

Oscar Ramos was the EDW team leader. The data warehouse resided on a cloud server and stored extensive business data, such as customer information, products, store, sales, and inventory, for the sole purpose of helping leaders of Parrl Inc. make informed business decisions. There were four other members of Oscar's team who, like him, were at the headquarters in the United States. The business also hired fifty software engineers as contractors to do the back-office work in the Philippines.

The team leader for the Reporting team was Jonathan Rogers. The team consisted of three full-time employees in the United States, including Jonathan, and twenty employees in the Philippines. Jonathan's team met with and interviewed the customers and gathered all the necessary inputs during the initial data gathering phase of the CRM and IM projects. This information was given to Oscar's team, which compiled, entered, and sorted all the data points into the Enterprise Data Warehouse. A data point for this project was information specifically related to a product purchased at stores or online, inventory data, and sales information. The Reporting team was then responsible for generating reports with the data available in the EDW.

Pointing the Finger

As the CRM project progressed, Oscar noticed that some data points were missing. He was agitated because missing data negatively affected the reliability of the sales reports reviewed by top management. These reports were also utilized by the other divisions/departments in the company to run their operations. The missing data problem most affected the sales and merchandising divisions – and developing the sales report was the responsibility of the Reporting team.

Oscar called Jonathan to tell him, "there are some missing data points from the project's first phase. We need that data as soon as possible before top management reviews the sales report." Jonathan confirmed that his team had gathered all the necessary data in the first phase without missing anything, but added, "Your EDW team may have mis-sorted or omitted data. Thus, your team will have to gather and re-sort the customer data." Oscar disagreed, saying, "We handled all the customer data given by your team with the utmost care and processed it to be available in the data warehouse. I firmly believe that the missing data is due to the incomplete information received from your team's meetings with the customers." Jonathan pointed out that there was no evidence that his team gathered incomplete information in the first phase. He asserted that the missing data should be the responsibility of the EDW team.

Oscar and Jonathan shared their reasoning with their respective teams, and the teams blamed each other for the missing data. Thus the project reached an impasse due to the conflict between the two IT teams. In the lunch room, members of Oscar's team got into a heated argument with a member of Jonathan's team concerning the missing data. The conflict primarily involved five individuals representing the two teams. Kevin learned of the dispute between the two teams from meeting with Oscar and Jonathan so he set up another meeting with them and instructed the three people who had the dispute in the lunch room to attend as well. During the meeting with all five employees, Kevin stated that the missing data had led to unreliable reports and thus delayed the official launch phase of the CRM and IM systems; the projects were behind schedule and top management was angry with the inaccurate sales reports. He wanted the missing data and the dispute resolved immediately, and in a way that it would not happen again.

Reflection Questions

1. What are the challenges of coordinating operations and business processes across teams?
2. What coordination or communication processes might have minimized the potential for conflict in this situation?

Learning Applications

1. Analyze this situation using two course concepts, frameworks, or models.
2. Think about an organization where you work or volunteer (or did so in the past). Describe a time when you experienced or observed a similar conflict over task responsibilities. What caused it and how was it handled?

Supplemental Readings

Razzetti, G. (2018). Want to resolve conflicts? Use this rule. www.fearlessculture. design/blog-posts/want-to-resolve-conflicts-use-this-rule

Schwarz, R. (2017). Is your team coordinating too much, or not enough? https://hbr. org/2017/03/is-your-team-coordinating-too-much-or-not-enough

Vitasek, K. (2023). 4 tips for building a "culture of collaboration" within your business. www.forbes.com/sites/katevitasek/2023/01/16/4-tips-for-building-a-culture-of-collabora tion-within-your-business

Case 10   Bias or Poor Training?

The Wine Train Incident

Monika L. Hudson and Keith O. Hunter

Synopsis

This case describes the issues leading up to the removal of Sistahs on the Reading Edge book club members from the Napa Valley Wine Train in August 2015. The club reserved and paid for seats a year in advance and noted they could be boisterous. The wine train company accepted their money and issued the tickets. The women's experience on the train deteriorated quickly and they were ejected by police at an unscheduled stop. Employees on the train had acted, but it was unclear whether their decisions were ones consistently made by the company or were biased. The story went viral with accusations toward the company that the women had been targeted for "laughing while Black."

Incident Onboard

Having warned book club members about noise as their coach left the Napa station and at least once more, an employee decided to exercise one of the more unpleasant aspects of the job – the group of women would be asked to leave the train at its next stop. The St. Helena police stood by to assure there were no problems related to the removal. As the train waited, security personnel escorted the women, a few who were elders and some who were crying, carefully down the aisles of the six train cars, following behind to assure there was no lingering. One of the train employees provided a small wooden stepladder and physically assisted the oldest member of the group down the stairs and out of the last car. The group huddled together, taking pictures as they waited for the taxi the train company provided to carry them back to Napa. Within a few hours, a company employee, who may or may not have witnessed the precipitating events, posted an explanation on the company's Facebook account as to why the women had been asked to leave.

Why did a celebratory gathering end with 11 members of a book club standing in a St. Helena parking lot on an August afternoon, having been evicted from the iconic Napa Valley Wine Train?

The Napa Valley Wine Train

Founded in 1864 by Vincent Michael DeDomenico, the Napa Valley Wine Train served as a tourist attraction offering fine wine and dining services to passengers as it

DOI: 10.4324/9781003326298-16

passed through the scenic backroads of California wine country. Its six antique 100-year-old railcars and 150-year-old rail corridor allowed the wine train to continue a transportation tradition that was disappearing from the American landscape. The Napa Valley Wine Train website indicated it was actually "one of the most distinctive Napa restaurants, offering a relaxing three-hour, 36-mile round-trip authentic, memorable experience that echoes the glory days of train travel, with fine dining service, multiple course meals, Napa Valley scenery and ultimate relaxation aboard exquisitely restored vintage rail cars" (Napa Valley Wine Train n.d.).

At the time of the incident, the company had 50+ employees providing direct service or handling general administration. Positions included such titles as group event manager, reservations assistant, car captain, and tour ambassador. All employees received general and specialized customer service training as well as education about the history of the company and its food and beverage offerings.

Sistahs on the Reading Edge Book Club

In 2015, the Sistahs on the Reading Edge book club had been around for 17 years. While the group was comprised mostly of African-American women, anyone could join; you just needed to be female, willing to both select and lead critical discussions of books, and interested in getting together on a regular basis with other like-minded women. Participants ranged in age from their late thirties to 83. The monthly gatherings frequently occurred in locations other than members' homes and the August 2015 session began like many others.

In the summer of 2014, after deciding it would provide a great backdrop for their monthly discussions, an August 2015 reservation was made for 15 members of the group to travel from Napa to St. Helena on the Napa Valley Wine Train. Lisa Johnson, a self-described speaker, coach, and self-made Sunshineologist, initiated the reservation. Via a posting to the Wine Train's electronic reservation system, Johnson noted that club members could get somewhat "boisterous" at times. She asked, in writing, if Sistahs on the Reading Edge could be seated in an area where their laughter and discussion would not disturb other travelers. Given that it was a year in advance of the trip, she expected her request could easily be accommodated.

The Violation: Laughing while Black

Saturday, August 22, 2015 began as a perfect day: sunny and warm with clear blue skies. Eleven of the book club members arrived ready to board the train at its Napa orientation. The photos and videos snapped on various cell phones, posted on Facebook prior to the trip, and subsequently shared with the press, show clusters of 5–6 women, smiling.

All the participants agreed that a Wine Train employee made a point of coming over and warning the book club group about disturbing others as they left the Napa station. While some book club members subsequently indicated they wondered why they were warned about noise even prior to the trip's getting under way, no points of contention apparently arose around that initial conversation.

About two hours into the journey, the group was again approached by train employees, citing complaints from other passengers about the noise level of the club's conversations. At this point, they were advised that their discussions and laughter had become a problem and they would need to leave. Some members reportedly asked if the situation could be resolved by relocating the group to a separate area away from other passengers; they were told that there was no space to accommodate this request.

The collective group of Sistahs on the Reading Edge club participants were then told they would be met at the train's St. Helena station, transported back to their cars in Napa at company expense, and provided with a full refund for the cost of their tickets. A few book club members protested they were no louder than others on the train, none of them were drunk and all were merely enjoying themselves in line with the wine train's stated purpose. However, as they readied themselves to leave the train car, another passenger reportedly scolded the group, stating "this is not a bar" (*Los Angeles Times*, August 25, 2015). According to a subsequent complaint posted on Lisa Johnson's Facebook page, train staff "paraded us through six cars on display in front of the other guests to waiting police like we were criminals" (*Reuters*, August 25, 2015).

The Virtual Backlash

Johnson wasted no time describing her and other club members' feelings about the incident on social national media, and the reaction was almost immediate. On that same Saturday afternoon, a train employee created a Facebook post, asserting that "following verbal and physical abuse toward other guests and staff, it was necessary to get our police involved" (Rocha, 2015). However, within hours, that particular company Facebook post was deleted.

By Sunday morning, a Twitter feed entitled hashtag #LaughingWhileBlack was trending, engendering sympathetic comments from the likes of Emory University political science professor Michael Lee Owens such as "race-based misophonia: a sound-induced disorder afflicting whites in the presence of black fun" (Skinner, 2015). By that Monday, over 13,000 signatures had been gathered via an on-line petition protesting the wine train employees' actions.

On Tuesday, August 25, still only two days after the original incident, a Latina UC-Berkeley student reported having posted Yelp information about a similar April 2015 experience, although she stipulated her party of 10 Latino individuals had only been threatened with action and not actually removed from the train:

> I think it was just that person complaining and then the manager, seeing that we were Latino, basically decided to discriminate [against] us because we were Latino and [a big] group ... I'm seeing a pattern. I'm realizing that how I was treated was not normal.
>
> (Stahl, 2015)

Later that day, wine train Chief Executive Officer Anthony Giaccio issued a written statement. indicating, "The Napa Valley Wine Train was 100 percent wrong in its handling of this issue. We accept full responsibility for our failures and for the chain of events that led to this regrettable treatment of our guests" (Skinner, 2015). Despite Giaccio's promise to have train employees participate in sensitivity training, book club members were not placated, particularly as they continued to feel the impact of the deleted Facebook post. For example, Lisa Carr, another of the women removed from the train, indicated members had dealt with a range of negative responses on social media, telling reporters, "It is horrible, it really is. People don't think that it is real. It's absolutely real ... People have been nasty. It's uncalled for" (Bhattacharjee, 2015).

By early October 2015, the Napa Valley Wine Train management was advised by its attorneys that book club members were considering pursuing legal action against the company. Considering the implications of legal action, what actions might company management have taken to ward off this type of negative next step?

Reflection Questions

1. Have you ever experienced conflict at work or as a customer that was escalated unnecessarily? What happened to cause that outcome? What could have been done differently?
2. Describe a time when you perceived a group being treated differently. What was the situation and how did others react or act in response? Could something have been done differently to improve the situation?

Learning Applications

1. Conduct an information interview with a manager. Ask how racial bias incidents in their workplace have been handled in the past, and also what the company or leadership has done (if anything) to minimize their occurrence. Is it viewed as successful?
2. Analyze the situation on the Wine Train using two course concepts, frameworks, or models so as to offer insights into what happened.

References

Bhattacharjee, R. (October 1, 2015). 11 Women kicked off Napa Valley Wine Train file $11 million racial discrimination suit. Accessed at: www.nbcbayarea.com/news/local/11-women-kicked-off-napa-valley-wine-train-file-11-million-racial-discrimination-suit/1979903/.

Napa Valley Wine Train. (n.d.) Tour our train cars. Retrieved July 14, 2023 from www.winetrain.com/tour-the-train/.

Rocha, V. (2015). Women kicked off Napa wine train says still humiliated despite apology. *Los Angeles Times*, August 25. Accessed at: www.latimes.com/local/lanow/la-me-ln-wine-train-apology-20150825-story.html.

Skinner, C. (2015). Black women booted from California wine train receive apology. Accessed at: www.reuters.com/article/idUSKCN0QU2F4/.

Stahl, J. (2015). The wine train thing happened to another group of passengers, this time Latino. Accessed at: https://slate.com/news-and-politics/2015/08/napa-valley-wine-train-discrimination-another-passenger-thinks-she-was-discriminated-against.html.

Supplemental Reading and Video

Eberhardt, J. L. (2020). How racial bias works – and how to disrupt it. Accessed at: www.ted.com/talks/jennifer_l_eberhardt_how_racial_bias_works_and_how_to_disrupt_it.

Oetting, J. (2020). 7 strategies for handling & resolving conflict with clients. Accessed at: https://blog.hubspot.com/agency/conflicts-clients.

Part IV
Managing Cross-Cultural Challenges

Part IV Introduction

The three cases in Part IV involve managing workers with different cultural expectations or practices. In Case 11 an immigrant entrepreneur faced challenges communicating and interacting with employees. The latter struggled to understand his accent, and had different expectations about the work environment. Case 12 focuses on the Australian CEO of Ellume Health and his hands-on leadership approach to the company's two teams of leaders working in Australia and in the US. Issues arose as the teams worked remotely and coordinated across a 14-hour time difference to handle the sudden exponential demand for the production, sale, and distribution of the product during the pandemic. Lastly, Case 13 deals with international etiquette issues faced by a US executive on a business trip to the Philippines. His Asian business associates invited him out for the evening and promised the entertainment would include something "typically Asian." After dinner, they ended up in a brothel for karaoke singing and "other services" at each participant's own discretion, which created a dilemma for Ben. The questions and readings below build on these themes of navigating cross-cultural workplace relationships and expectations.

Part IV Cases

Case 11, "Culture Clash and the Unraveling of an Immigrant Entrepreneur's American Dream," looks at the experiences of a Bangladeshi immigrant who prepared for and then opened two fast-food franchise businesses in the United States. The owner faced challenges related to communicating, managing, training, and operating an American-based business as his expectations differed from the US employees' expectations and perceptions about their work attitudes, loyalty, and the use of family members in leadership roles.

The learning objectives for this case include:

- Evaluate the value of understanding cultural differences in workplace communication and management.
- Assess the importance of building quality relationships with employees and team members.
- Assess the impact of communication and the interpersonal competency on the success of a businesses.
- Recognize factors that may impact intercultural management.

DOI: 10.4324/9781003326298-17

Case 12, "Trust and Communication Across Borders: Leadership Challenges at Ellume Health," focuses on the founder and CEO of Australian-based Ellume Health as he struggled to manage two teams of leaders working remotely in Australia and in the US. The company was an early provider of at-home rapid tests for COVID-19 and became a key supplier to the US government and major corporate distributors. Cross-cultural issues arose as the teams worked remotely and coordinated across a 14-hour time difference to handle the production, sale, and distribution of the test kits. The founder struggled to maintain his hands-on leadership approach as US demand for the product exceeded the production capacity in Australia.

The learning objectives for this case include:

- Analyze situational factors and recommend contingent adaptations of leadership styles.
- Identify cross-cultural factors affecting interdependent virtual teams working from different countries.

Case 13, "When in Rome (or Manila ...): Where Business, Law, and Ethics Meet," deals with the international etiquette issues faced by a US executive on a business trip to the Philippines. Ben was invited by his Asian business associates to an evening of entertainment, including something identified as "typically Asian". After dinner, the men ended up in a brothel for an evening of karaoke singing. It also became clear to Ben that "other services" were included at each participant's own discretion. Ben's situation and his decisions involved legal, ethical, and business perspectives.

The learning objectives for this case include:

- Identify reasons that may lead a person to accept potentially unethical or illegal behavior in a business or peer-pressure environment.
- Apply an ethical framework to the cultural differences of doing business overseas.
- Use an ethics quick check and create a potential exit/response strategy when confronted with a similar dilemma.

Part IV Supplemental Questions

Reflection Questions

1.   Think of a country you would enjoy working in for one or more years. How does the business culture there differ from that of your home country? Other than language skills, what would be the most challenging cross-cultural aspect for you to adapt to in the business environment in that country?
2.   Consider a time when you worked in a group or project with someone who seemed to have a different cultural background than yourself. What attitudes, behaviors, or expectations did the two of you have that seemed to be different or similar? What aspects of the overall situation aided in or diminished your ability to worked together effectively?

Discussion Questions

1. How might a manager assigned to oversee employees from a different culture go about preparing for that role?
2. What challenges might employees encounter when their manager is from a different culture? What would be the difficulties they would face in trying to resolve some of those challenges?
3. What is the responsibility (or role) of the company in preparing a manager who will oversee employees who are from a different culture? Does a company have ongoing responsibility after any initial managerial preparation or training?

Part IV Related Readings and Video

Working across Cultures

Henman, M. (2023). From conflict to cooperation: Building stronger cross-cultural teams. Accessed at: www.business.com/articles/from-conflict-to-cooperation-building-stronger-cross-cultural-teams/

Kennedy, J. C. (2018). Forbearance of culturally inappropriate leadership behaviors: A conceptual model. *Journal of Global Mobility: The Home of Expatriate Management Research*, 6(1), 4–19. Accessed at: https://doi.org/10.1108/JGM-04-2017-0016

Worthy, C. (2023). How can we work together with people from different cultures? Accessed at: www.youtube.com/watch?v=6u_HirSvl5o

Managing across Cultures

Brett, J. M., Behfar, K. J., & Kern, M. (2006). Managing multicultural teams. *Harvard Business Review*, 84(11), 84–91. Accessed at: https://hbr.org/2006/11/managing-multicultural-teams

Knight, R. (2015). How to run a meeting of people from different cultures. *Harvard Business Review*, December 4. Accessed at: https://hbr.org/2015/12/how-to-run-a-meeting-of-people-from-different-cultures

Meyer, E. (2016). How to lead a successful international team. Accessed at: www.youtube.com/watch?v=Q3X7legs3gM

Rowland, D. (2016). Leading across cultures requires flexibility and curiosity. *Harvard Business Review*, May 30. Accessed at: https://hbr.org/2016/05/leading-across-cultures-requires-flexibility-and-curiosity

Case 11 Culture Clash

The Unraveling of an Immigrant Entrepreneur's American Dream

Rifat Mahmud, Joy A. Jones and Elizabeth A. McCrea

Synopsis

This case describes a Bangladeshi immigrant's experiences owning and operating two American-based fast-food franchise locations in the United States, from the perspective of his son. It relates the challenges the franchisee faced in communicating, managing, training, and operating an American-based business when his cultural expectations were different from those of his employees and of the franchisor.

An Uncomfortable Situation

"Hello, may I help you?" Riyadh Ahmed smiled as he stood patiently behind the service counter, ready to enter the customer's food order. The swinging door to the kitchen was closed behind him, but some noise still seeped through. Riyadh continued to focus on the customer.

"Umm …" the customer said, as she craned her neck to view the menu board that hung over the counter.

Suddenly the noise level coming from the kitchen increased. Riyadh could hear his father, Hasan Ahmed, arguing in Bengali, and his mother, Nordia Ahmed, responding in kind. He ignored it. He was used to the way his parents discussed both business and personal family issues at work – usually at top volume. They were both under a lot of stress due to the decline in the franchise business, so discussions of even mundane, everyday issues often escalated to what to American ears sounded like shouting matches.

Still facing the customer, Riyadh could see that she was uneasy about the noise emanating from the kitchen, so he smiled again and tried to convey a relaxed attitude. "How can I help you today?" he asked again, pleasantly, in a soft tone. "Umm." She glanced nervously at the sounds coming from behind the kitchen door. "Never mind," she replied, as she turned and left the fast-food restaurant without ordering.

Since the dining area was now empty, Riyadh turned, pushed the door open and glanced into the kitchen. What should have been a bustling workspace with a team of kitchen staff was peopled by his mother, his father, and two nonfamily members: a cook and a dishwasher. The cook did not even look up when the kitchen door opened. He kept his eyes focused on the pickup orders he was slowly preparing. His tense shoulders and stiff body language signaled that he felt uncomfortable. The dishwasher spoke very little English and no Bengali, so he merely ignored the conflict and continued with his work.

DOI: 10.4324/9781003326298-18

"Ammu. Abbu. We can hear you out front," Riyadh said, addressing his parents. His mother turned to face Riyadh and switched to English. Riyadh was fluent in Bengali, of course, but the more time he spent in the United States, the more comfortable he felt with English. Both of his parents were also proficient in English, but his father's strong accent sometimes made it difficult for Americans to understand him. "Abbu doesn't understand," his mother said. "It is not like at home in Bangladesh when he had his own business. Here he must follow the rules the franchisor sets, or we will be in violation of the contract!"

"How am I supposed to save the business if I don't bend the rules at least a little?" Hasan replied in English. "This tactic worked for my business in Bangladesh. Why wouldn't it work here?" His mother threw up her hands in frustration.

Out of the corner of his eye, Riyadh saw the cook's shoulders relax. *He probably thought they were talking about him,* Riyadh thought. Hasan often slipped into Bengali when speaking with his family members at the restaurant. It was their first language after all, and it was easier to convey complex ideas or speak about personal family matters in Bengali. Riyadh knew employees often wondered *what* or even *who* they were talking about right in front of them and it made them uncomfortable.

As much as Riyadh tried to explain American culture to his parents, they often did not get it. For example, he had told them that some gestures that were normal in Bangladesh were considered offensive here. For example, his father often pointed directly at employees when speaking to them, which, in Bangladesh, is normal. However, Americans found it quite aggressive and offensive.

Riyadh's father got frustrated with his employees. Hasan's strong accent often made him hard to understand and his tone was often perceived as hostile. When the workers couldn't understand him, they naturally asked him to repeat himself. But his father often thought they understood perfectly well and were just making fun of him.

Hasan expected the kind of seriousness, loyalty, and deference from the staff here in America that he had received from his employees in Bangladesh. But a job in a fast-food restaurant was often just a stepping-stone for American employees. The normal turnover rate in the fast-food industry – the rate at which employees leave jobs – had been estimated to be as high as 150% per year for these low-skilled positions (Rosenbaum, 2019). This cost owners money. The National Restaurant Association estimated it cost as much as $2,000 to find, hire, and train a new fast-food employee.

The more frustrated Hasan got, the more he relied on his family. Nordia was the assistant manager, and his two teenaged children worked part-time during the school year and full-time in the summer. Employees felt that he showed his family favoritism, but what was he supposed to do? Hasan trusted his family and knew he could count on them – much more than the unreliable American workers who quit so often.

Hasan believed that the rules that were a part of his franchise contract hindered his entrepreneurial spirit. He had many innovative ideas to grow the business, like new menu items and promotional tactics, but they were either forbidden or had to be approved by the corporate office – a bureaucratic process that took months. This meant Hasan couldn't implement new ideas on a timely basis, ideas that might have turned the struggling business around.

To compound matters, the franchisor required new promotional or marketing tactics every six months or so, even though they didn't always fit with Hasan's local environment. As per the contract, the entire cost burden for these programs fell to the franchisees. These added expenses further exacerbated the financial challenges of his struggling business.

The situation seemed hopeless, and Riyadh didn't know what he could do to make the situation better for his family.

A Promising Start

In Bangladesh, Hasan Ahmed was already a successful business owner and family man at the age of 29. But he longed to become an entrepreneur in the United States, where he felt he could go even further. It was his own American Dream. His opportunity came in 2005, when he legally immigrated to the United States. His wife, Nordia, and his two young children, Ryma and Riyadh, joined him on this new adventure.

After arriving in America, Hasan had been eager to build his American Dream. But going from being his own boss to someone else's employee was not an easy transition, especially in a new culture. Hasan was determined to succeed, and he worked hard. After various roles – including kitchen worker, assistant manager, and general manager – in several small food businesses, he was offered a kitchen position at a famous pizza chain's franchise location. He got along great with the franchise unit's owner and Hasan worked his way up to a managerial position within six months.

In his first year as a manager, the franchise location's sales increased by 20–25%. Hasan hired Nordia as a shift manager, and that contributed further to smooth operations. The following year, sales increased another 10–15%. At that point the store was one of the top five highest grossing stores for the chain in the state. After three years, the franchise owner was so impressed with Hasan's managerial performance that he recommended him to the corporate office as a potential new franchisee in 2014. After going through the rigorous qualification process to purchase a unit, Ahmed mortgaged his family's home and put everything he had into starting the new business.

Franchisee training

Once approved to purchase a franchise unit, Hasan attended the mandatory franchisee training program at the chain's corporate headquarters in March of 2016. The three-month program was rigorous as the potential franchise owners were required to learn the company's culture, values, brand promise, products and services, employee evaluation system, policies, and procedures.

Hasan felt at a significant disadvantage compared to his peers. The instructors assumed that all the trainees were well-versed in U.S. business practices and terminology – practices and terminology that were foreign to Hasan. This was worsened by language barriers. Although Hasan was proficient in English, he did not understand the many technical terms, idioms, and subtle nuances in the documents and lectures. Despite these challenges, he successfully completed the training and achieved the required passing scores of 80 percent or above on all the company's assessments.

As comprehensive as it was, the training program missed some key elements that would have helped Hasan be more successful. It did not include a clear discussion of American-based business practices, policies, and procedures. It did not prepare participants for the transition from the role of manager to owner. While a manager can focus solely on day-to-day operations, an owner must be more strategic. Long-term planning, monitoring the local business environment, setting goals and then designing plans to achieve them, and other strategic skills were also not included in the program. Retention – both of customers and trained employees – was an important contributor to franchisee success, but exactly how to achieve retention was not explicitly discussed. Finally, the training did not include the essential "soft" skills an owner needs for success, such as culturally appropriate communication, adaptability, confidence, teamwork, and negotiations.

Upon completing the training program, Hasan was finally poised to attain his dream of owning a business in the United States. He spent time finding a good location, ordering equipment and supplies, and hiring approximately ten full-time employees. These employees – shift leaders, cashiers, and cooks – ranged in age from 16 years old to 30 years old. As when he was a manager, Hasan did his best to ensure that the individuals had prior relevant experience. Once hired, Hasan trained the new employees and his family members in the systems and processes laid out by the franchisor. Nordia, was the assistant manager, and his children, Riyadh and Ryma learned the shift leader role, even though they were still in high school and younger than most of the staff.

The Grand Opening was held in May of 2016. It was literally a dream come true. Like many new restaurants, there were some challenges in starting up and there were some operational difficulties to work out. Despite its nationally known brand identity, he struggled to build a clientele in the new location.

The Dream Unraveled

Despite his high hopes and driving work ethic, Hasan faced multiple challenges within six months of the grand opening. Riyadh noticed that at times, employees did not understand his father due to his strong accent. When conveying instructions, important information was lost in translation. Both the employees and Hasan got frustrated by this communications barrier, especially during busy times in the restaurant. Employees repeatedly asked clarifying questions, and Hasan raised his voice as if increasing the volume helped. Then the workers felt like they had been yelled at, which made the situation worse.

Meanwhile, Hasan felt they did not respect his authority, and he became irritated and indignant. The workers either stopped asking questions, or, in some cases, they quit. In these situations, Riyadh explained to his father that he should have assumed that the worker was sincere, and just calmly repeat himself, perhaps using different words, if an employee wanted clarification.

Riyadh also noticed that some workers enjoyed joking around while they worked. They felt it made the time go faster and it made the workplace more fun. But to Hasan, the restaurants represented his hopes and dreams and, most importantly, his family's future. It was serious business, not a playground. The joking did not sit well with him, and he often tried to squash it. As someone who straddled both cultures, Riyadh felt his father was too serious and did not understand the American work culture.

Further complicating matters, within a year after his business launched, a nearby franchise unit became available. Although his first unit was not firmly established yet, Hasan felt he couldn't pass up the opportunity to expand, so he purchased a second store across town. Opening a second location within the first year of ownership more than doubled Hasan's workload. He had to divide his time between the two establishments, adding an extra layer of complexity. He worked almost seven days a week, from open to close. He even kept a pillow in his office so he could catch an occasional nap during the long twelve-hour days.

As sales declined and financial constraints arose, Hasan reduced the hours of the paid employees and allocated more hours to his family members. Nordia was on a salary, so extra hours for her did not increase costs and Ryma and Riyadh were unpaid. After these changes, Riyadh observed increased tardiness, neglect of stringent cleaning procedures, a reluctance to upsell, and a general lack of productivity among the nonfamily employees.

In addition, whenever Hasan had to be absent from one of the restaurants, he put one of his family members in charge. The decision did not sit well with the other employees; they perceived it as favoritism. Riyadh overheard employees grumbling that they shouldn't bother trying harder because they would never have a chance to get promoted. This attitude surprised Hasan because he was not intentionally showing favoritism, and he did not expect his workers to feel this way. He merely felt it was imperative for his family members to play an essential role in his businesses, and, in his absence, he was more comfortable when they were in charge.

Sales continued to decline in both franchise locations. As morale continued to sink, and employees left, Hasan grew increasingly frustrated at the time he needed to spend finding and training replacements instead of focusing on operations and strategy. To improve the business financials, he stopped taking a salary, but that made the family's personal situation precarious. Riyadh recalled, "My father was under so much stress and there never seemed enough time to course correct. There may have been resources available to him from corporate, but Hasan did not even have time to research or implement any possible changes."

Riyadh hated to see that his father's dream was unraveling. Was there something more he or his sister, Ryma, could do? What advice could he give?

Reflection Questions

1. Describe a time when you experienced or observed a situation that involved coworkers or managers from different cultures. Identify aspects of the situation that were helpful in communicating with employees and aspects that made it difficult. In retrospect, what should have been done differently to increase the effectiveness of the interactions?
2. What responsibility do you think the franchisor should have to provide cultural training to entrepreneurs who pay for the rights to open and run a franchised business? What cultural immersion training do franchisees need, and who should pay for it?

Learning Applications

1. Analyze this situation using two course concepts, frameworks, or models.
2. Research and summarize several communication or coordination processes that help to minimize potential conflict when managing employees who are from different cultural backgrounds.
3. Compare the national culture of Bangladesh to the US or to another country and identify similarities and differences. This may be a helpful site: https://geerthof stede.com/culture-geert-hofstede-gert-jan-hofstede/6d-model-of-national-culture/.

Reference

Rosenbaum, E. (2019). Panera is losing nearly 100% of its workers every year as fast-food turnover crisis worsens. Accessed at: www.cnbc.com/2019/08/29/fast-food-restaurants-in-america-are-losing-100percent-of-workers-every-year.html.

Supplemental Readings

Culture Factor Group. (n.d.) Intercultural management: What you need to know. Accessed at: www.hofstede-insights.com/.

Elkins, K. (2015). These fascinating diagrams reveal how to manage people in different countries. Accessed at: www.businessinsider.com/how-to-manage-people-in-other-countries-2015-3 (based on a book by Richard D. Lewis, *Cross-Cultural Communication: A Visual Approach*, Transcreen Publications, 2nd revised edition 2008).

Case 12   Trust and Communication across Borders

Leadership Challenges at Ellume Health

George C. Kokoros and Laurie L. Levesque

Synopsis

The founder and CEO of Australian-based Ellume Health struggled to manage two teams of leaders working remotely in Australia and in the US. The company was an early provider of at-home rapid tests for COVID-19 and became a key supplier to the US government and major corporate distributors. The teams worked remotely and coordinated across a 14-hour time difference to handle the production, sale, and distribution of the test kits. The founder struggled as US demand for the product exceeded the production capacity in Australia.

Culture Clash or More?

It was a bright autumn morning in April 2020 in Brisbane, Australia as Dr. Sean Parsons sat in his home office and wondered how to manage a rapidly growing business and his two leadership teams in the United States and Australia, separated by a 14-hour time difference and pandemic travel bans. He started his 12-hour days early to accommodate the US time zones as a small window of time between 4:00 and 7:00 p.m. EST (6:00–9:00 a.m. AEST) was acceptable for synchronous meetings. Parsons attended many meetings that addressed functional decisions across the two continents and was responsible for company strategy. His Australian employees were tired of waking up early to meet with their American counterparts. Both sides grumbled about not fully knowing what the others worked on during the part of the day when they were not online together. Parsons faced a critical decision that would have lasting effects on his goal to scale Ellume Health to successfully incorporate the American market: "How can I get these two teams to work together more effectively? Should I move critical management functions to the US leadership team and redefine the role of our Australian headquarters?"

Ellume Health Background

Ellume Health was born out of the idea that people should be able to get faster access to diagnosis and treatment for infectious diseases. During the swine flu epidemic in 2009, Dr. Parsons worked in the emergency department at Brisbane Memorial Hospital, where he watched hundreds of symptomatic people flood the lobby daily

DOI: 10.4324/9781003326298-19

seeking an official diagnosis. Parsons wondered, "Why should all these infected and uninfected people be mixing together in our lobby?" spreading disease if they could be triaged prior to arriving at the hospital. He knew at-home testing would solve this, but effective tests were unavailable commercially. So, he took on the mission to develop a technology simple enough for the average person to use at home to confirm whether they were positive or negative for the flu.

Parsons had no significant business experience, but knew that a medical test-device venture required a team of talented employees. He had launched Ellume Health in 2016 with his wife Mia as the Chief Marketing Officer (CMO), building on her past experience at a consumer products company. He recruited people he knew to the team: scientists, regulators, lab techs, engineers and others with manufacturing experience, and another friend who invested the majority of the start-up funding. The team worked to create a reliable device that could be used effectively by the general public. The process was slow; each step involved clinical trials and updated prototypes. Ellume licensed the underlying technology to a company for tuberculosis testing in Africa and other countries where the disease was prevalent. Concurrently, Ellume neared reaching its goal: an at-home flu test. Parsons was smart and well-spoken, and involved in every facet of the business. His down-to-earth charismatic presence allowed him to connect easily and build key relationships with potential buyers. He showed the prototype to decision-makers from the US Food and Drug Administration (FDA) and immediately realized that the largest market was in the US. Ellume's presence in that market would determine the company's success. Then the COVID-19 pandemic arrived.

Pivoting and Fast Growth

Labs in the US were unable to handle the demand for COVID-19 tests, thus the only viable solution was to supplement with at-home testing. The US Department of Defense (DOD) contacted Parsons and asked that Ellume pivot from a device that provided a flu diagnosis to one that rapidly diagnosed COVID-19. The growing death toll in the US contributed to a sense of urgency. Parson's executive team worked with the FDA to qualify for an emergency use authorization (EUA) to sell a home rapid antigen COVID-19 test. Granted in spring 2021, it rapidly catapulted Ellume from research and development into full scale production in Australia. The DOD ordered millions of tests with staggered delivery dates. CVS Health and Amazon wanted to sell Ellume's test and requested immediate delivery of millions of test kits. The first shipments were flown from Australia to the US in June 2021.

Leading from Down Under

Although Ellume's headquarters and manufacturing were in Australia, the majority of sales were half a world away. Parsons frequently wondered "How the hell are we going to handle all of this new business?" There were no systems in place or business processes in his small company to manage the explosive demand. Parsons and the Australian team oversaw product development, operations, supply chain management, sales, marketing, human resources, and finance. Even with US retail experience, the Australian who managed US sales and marketing found it difficult and unwieldy to address the nuances and preferences of consumers in a complex market located 7,500 miles away. The 14-hour time difference made reaching customers during business hours almost impossible. Much communication was therefore asynchronous through email, which left issues open-ended or slow to resolve. It was expensive but necessary to have subject matter experts available in the right time zone, so Ellume employed consultants in the US. This expanded team worked long hours across time zones and made decisions daily about raw material purchase, shipping, contracts with retailers, and capacity issues scaling manufacturing. The US government told Parsons it could no longer rely on production so far away and Ellume needed a manufacturing presence in the US; it contributed financing to help Ellume build a facility in Frederick, Maryland (USA).

Coordinating across Continents

Parsons realized that to be effective some coordination needed to be in the US. He decided which functional areas to keep in Brisbane and which to delegate to the quickly hired "US leadership team," which managed Ellume USA, LLC. Their main focus was on business development, customer service, and sales (see Figure 12.1). Ellume's "US president" was a soft-spoken and thoughtful Australian scientist with a background in operations, manufacturing, and distribution, though not in fast-growth organizations. He ran the weekly all-hands meetings, and the US employees respected him as someone who got things done. Together with the CMO and a new VP of

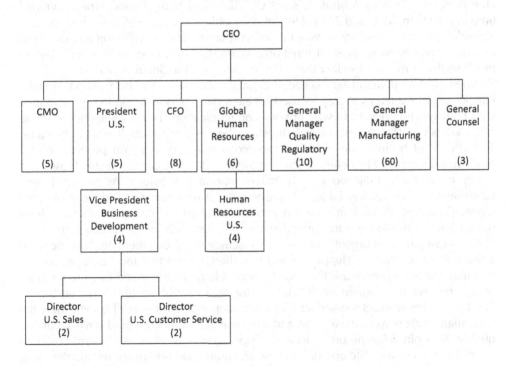

Note: parentheses denote number of employees in that unit

Figure 12.1 Ellume Health organizational chart.

business development, he interviewed, selected, and hired eight more US employees, including a director of sales and VP of human resources.

While the US employees worked remotely from their homes, the Frederick facility was under construction. They met their Australian counterparts for the first time in a virtual meeting, and most never met in person. Informal conversation was minimal at the start of the weekly meetings; the Australians eschewed the American's practice of talking about personal lives or social topics prior to the meeting. Some Australian employees arrived late as they had to leave other meetings to make time for the meetings with the US team. Due to the many conflicting meetings, it was not uncommon for them to show up and cut off mid-sentence those who had been chatting to say "let's go, let's stay on track" and jump right into the agenda. The Australians questioned the US team's effectiveness at handling the unrelenting demand for the product, asking if they could manage customers' expectations better. They didn't understand the US market and asked so many questions about the US team's actions and decisions that the latter felt everything they did was second-guessed. Complicating matters was that the US team was asleep during much of the standard Australian business hours, and vice versa. Those precious overlap hours when meetings could happen between employees in the two countries became even more critical as the company grew.

Decisions on many fronts moved at a rapid pace and there was little time to develop systems to manage the business more efficiently. To the US executives, discussions about labor, raw materials, and capacity seemed slow to progress to actionable decisions. Due to Australia's strict COVID travel bans, Parsons spent minimal time in the US in 2020 and 2021. He met daily online with the entire leadership team regardless of which country he was in, and constantly faced conflicting interests from executives representing different functions. Many decisions were made every day, so much so that it masked the fact that some could impact a global pandemic.

When product demand far exceeded capacity and there was no solution in sight, Parsons urged the teams to stay focused on each day's priorities and to be disciplined with both synchronous and asynchronous communication. The complexities of filling sales orders were the subject of daily meetings between the Australian and US teams. The US VP of business development needed frequent updates on production and product availability. He believed the Australians did not communicate those in a timely manner and took too long to make important decisions. As the US manufacturing was not yet available, he pushed the Australians to produce more and repeatedly asked, "Why can't we run two manufacturing shifts per day so our lines run 24 hours a day to meet this new demand?" The Australians either countered with, "Why is everything so urgent?" or deferred discussions by commenting, "Let me have a think about it." Parsons stepped in and told the US team that increased production was impossible, "I cannot ask them to do more. I had already asked them to ramp up once when we transitioned to COVID-19 testing. I cannot double down on them." The factory flex workers worked varying hours depending on need. Parsons knew the Australian workers were maxed out and any increase in speed would have sacrificed quality. As a physician he understood that poor quality medical equipment could be the difference between life and death. Indeed, Ellume had one major recall after using a batch of flawed processing fluid from a vendor. The company had ramped up so quickly to meet demand for COVID-19 home tests in that first year that it had been unable to screen all the components from vendors as thoroughly as it had previously.

Parsons met every day with the sales executives and perceived a growing tension between the US and Australian teams. The Australians were very deliberate in making decisions; the US employees wanted faster decisions. In a bi-weekly production planning meeting, as the director of production explained the limited capacity available for the next 30 days, the entire Australian operations team nodded, seemingly in sync with his numbers. While reviewing production forecasts, the Australians commented that their US counterparts failed to manage customer expectations. The US team criticized the Australians as laid-back and satisfied with losing millions in potential sales. The US director of commercial sales expressed concerns that, "We are continuing to lose sales because there is no real sense of urgency from the Australian team." The woman who hired him quit three months later without another job to jump to, and told him that she felt that the Australians did not listen to her and constantly spoke down to her. The US team felt hamstrung by what they perceived as slow decision-making; a few other team members quit shortly after being hired. The human resources staff had difficulty attracting experienced talent needed to manage the US business, so their recruitment focus shifted to bring in talent who could improve systems and work together across continents.

Production scaled down and contractors and flex/temporary employees were let go when worldwide demand dropped off suddenly in July and August 2021 as people worldwide temporarily resumed their "normal lives." Then COVID-19 cases from the Delta variant ballooned and demand for tests skyrocketed; Walmart, Amazon, CVS, Target, Walgreens, and other customers grew impatient with unfilled orders. The Australian leaders balked, feared that ramping up would create production fluctuations and trigger employment issues for the manufacturing plant's flex workforce, who had worked hard and then been let go.

The Path Forward

Parsons knew there was no substitute for his home test other than laboratory testing, and their delayed lab results caused healthy people to be unnecessarily exposed. COVID-19 catapulted what had been a business on a slow steady path to one with expedited FDA approval and full production in under 30 days. This explosive growth brought with it many issues. On Parsons's mind was how to get the two executive teams to work together effectively when they were from two different countries and everyone worked remotely. While the US manufacturing facility was under construction, sales orders exceeded the Australian factory capacity. It was unsustainable and he realized it was imperative to solve Ellume's growing leadership challenges. He also knew that his decisions about Ellume would have a profound impact on how the trajectory of the pandemic affected people's lives.

Reflection Questions

1. What are the challenges of managing a virtual team?
2. What can leaders do to mitigate the challenges of team members working across time zones?
3. How should founders adapt their leadership style as their company grows?

Learning Applications

1. Analyze this situation using two course concepts, frameworks, or models.

2.   Research best practices for managing virtual teams and develop a list of strategies for fostering respectful and inclusive decision-making and collaboration.

Supplemental Readings

Jules, C., Kshirsagar, A., & Lloyd George, K. L. (2022). Scaling up: How founder CEOs and teams can go beyond aspiration to ascent. Accessed March 13, 2023 at: www.mckinsey.com/capabilities/people-and-organizational-performance/our-insights/scaling-up-how-founder-ceos-and-teams-can-go-beyond-aspiration-to-ascent

Lobell, K. O. (2023). How to best lead a multicultural or international team. Accessed March 13, 2023 at: www.businessnewsdaily.com/8211-expand-business-internationally.html

Case 13   When in Rome (or Manila ...)

Where Business, Law, and Ethics Meet

Ralf Mehnert-Meland

Synopsis

On a business trip to the Philippines, Ben was invited by his Asian business associates to an evening of entertainment, including something "typically Asian." After dinner, the men ended up in a brothel. Unbeknown to Ben, the purpose of the visit was an evening of karaoke singing. It was also clear that "other services" were included at each participant's own discretion.

Overseas Assignment

Ben Rasmussen[1] was a young mid-level international business development manager with a quickly growing software company in the midwestern United States and happily married. He and his wife had just had their first child in June. It was now early July, and Ben found himself on a business trip to the Philippines. Ben had successfully identified and recruited his company's first independent distributor in the Asian market, located in the Philippines. He now had been invited to the capital Manila to present at the main conference introducing the company's software products. This was a very important event to launch the products in Asia which the company viewed as a significant growth area in its overall global business expansion. It was also an important stepping stone for his personal career. He was the only company representative at the event and his successful presence would likely result in additional business opportunities for the company. He had already traveled to several countries around the world, but never to Asia. His approach to business – and to life – was simple. Ben was a straight shooter: What you saw is what you got. Ben did not lie or cheat, and he followed the rules. His approach was about to face a major test on this assignment.

After flying over 22 hours from the United States and crossing the international date line, Ben landed at Ninoy Aquino International Airport in Manila very late in the evening. The airport was extremely busy. Fortunately, Mr. James Chang, the managing director and owner of the Philippine distributor and organizer of the event, had arranged VIP treatment for Ben. Someone waited inside the secured area to pick Ben up and whisk him through customs and immigration. Ben never showed his passport, stood in line or even saw a government official in the process. A car and driver were waiting to drive him to his hotel in the Makati Central Business District.

The next day, Ben explored the immediate neighborhoods around his hotel. He had spent a restless night, dealing with the 14-hour time difference. On his walks, he was

DOI: 10.4324/9781003326298-20

immediately confronted with the sights, sounds and smells of a vastly different culture. Being from a northern climate, he also began feeling the effects of the time-lag, lack of sleep and the unfamiliar near-equatorial hot and humid tropical climate.

Building Business Relationships after Hours

After another night with little sleep, Ben presented at the New World Makati Hotel. He was one of three keynote speakers and his presentation was very well received by the attendees. Ben was convinced that the positive reception was an indication of the great potential for the company's products in the Philippines. At the end of the conference day, he was ready to leave for the hotel to catch up on his sleep when the conference organizer said: "Ben, as a thank you for making the long trip and presenting, I would be honored if you could join me and the other speakers tonight for dinner. I will have a driver pick you up at the hotel at 6:30 p.m." Despite his fatigue, Ben did not feel he could turn down the invitation and agreed to join.

The group enjoyed a wonderful dinner and drinks at a high-end Chinese restaurant. In addition to the two other speakers, who worked for potential partner companies in Tokyo and Hong Kong, two of James's employees had joined them. The dinner wrapped up at about 10 p.m. when James asked the group to join him in "something typically Asian." Two cars picked up the men to drive to a different location. Ben fell asleep during the 30-minute drive. He woke up when the car stopped, and his door was opened. As he groggily stepped out of the car, he realized that he did not know where he was or how to get back to his hotel. He also noticed a row of brightly lit buildings. Led by James, the group entered the largest of these buildings.

Crossing the threshold and assessing the set-up and décor of the interior, Ben immediately realized that they had just entered a brothel. The entire lobby was red, from the lights on the walls to the carpet and the furniture. Right in front of the group, on red leather couches, sat 20 of the most beautiful women Ben had ever seen. The owner of the establishment greeted James with the words: "Welcome back. We have prepared everything as you requested." He then guided the group into a small side room with a U-shaped low seating arrangement and a table full of food and drink.

Ben was given the place of honor at the head of the table. At this point, he was extremely uncomfortable as he had not expected – and did not want – to be in this situation. After the men were seated, James asked the owner to "bring in the women." He then turned to Ben with the words: "Ben, you have first pick. Pick your woman." After assuring James that he was "just fine without one," James strongly insisted on his request. Ben selected one of the women, who immediately proceeded to sit extremely close to his right side. James then insisted that Ben needed a second woman, picked her, and sat her extremely close to Ben's left side.

Ben was in a state of panic. He did not know where he was or how to find a way out of this situation. He was seated between two extremely attractive women whose obvious goal was to make sure he was going to have an enjoyable evening. While he had no conceptual problem with legal prostitution, he did not want to be in this situation, being happily married with a newborn at home. Ben also was unsure whether prostitution was legal in the Philippines. In addition, Ben's company had recently put in place its first employee policy regarding acceptable business behavior and ethical expectations. The policy clearly prohibited illegal behavior, such as bribery and harassment. It was, however, somewhat vague with regard to other activities by generally stating that employees had to conduct themselves in a "business-like manner while conducting business for the company." Ben was not sure whether his presence at this event could be construed as business-like behavior or as a violation of that policy.

After all the men had been paired up with women, James informed the group with a wink that "everything was included" and that "other options" were available to those who did not enjoy the company of women. The women started serving the drinks and food and began conversation with their respective patrons. Ben found his companions to be extremely well-spoken and educated.

"Something Typically Asian"

At some time, what was referred to as the "typically Asian" part of the evening started. A curtain at the far end of the room was opened to display a large TV screen. Several microphones were provided. The group spent the rest of the night until about 4:30 in the morning singing karaoke. The main role of the women was to animate the men to sing and enjoy their evening out. Ben knew that karaoke singing in business settings had long been a fixture of Asian business culture. Drinking and spending evenings in front of a microphone is seen as a way to unwind, build trust across language and cultural barriers, and facilitate business dealings. After realizing the true purpose of the invitation in the evening, Ben found himself much more relaxed and enjoying the company.

There was no question that the men could have enjoyed all the other services that were "included" per James's statement earlier in the evening. That, however, was for each participant to decide on his own.

Reflection Questions

1. Think of a time when you felt pressured to go along with a group in a decision that you were against. What was the situation and how did the decision relate to your personal ethics? How did you respond?
2. It is normal to experience discomfort and anxiety when travelling to other regions or countries. To what extent should you accommodate your behavior and expectations to local customs and norms when traveling? Is this the same if you are traveling for business purposes?

Learning Applications

1. Analyze this situation using two course concepts, frameworks, or models.
2. Choose a country other than one you have lived in and research its business etiquette norms. Identify three that would be more challenging for you to adapt to and explain why.

Supplemental Readings and Video

Cairl, V. (2017). 5 rules for karaoke (and how it helps office culture). Accessed at: www.linkedin.com/pulse/5-rules-karaoke-how-helps-office-culture-victoria-cairl/

Middleton, J. (2015). Cultural intelligence: the competitive edge for leaders. Accessed at: www.youtube.com/watch?v=izeiRjUMau4

Weinstein, B. (2017). What's the difference between business etiquette and business ethics? Accessed at: www.forbes.com/sites/bruceweinstein/2017/11/28/whats-the-difference-between-business-etiquette-and-business-ethics

Acknowledgement

This case was originally published in 2018 in the *International Journal of Instructional Cases* and is reprinted here with permission of the publisher and author.

Note

1 Names and specific locations have been anonymized.

Part V

Motivating Subordinates and Fostering Engagement

Part V Introduction

Part V offers three cases focused on the issues of engaging and retaining quality workers. In Case 14 the founder of a PR firm struggles to change the trend of employee turnover. While some approaches are counter to the industry norms, others are based on her beliefs about what should work. Case 15 introduces the complexities of working with colleagues whose motivation and follow-through differ markedly from one's own. Being a team leader with peers presents unique challenges when it comes to motivating fair contributions for the credit claimed for work. The theme of employee retention is revisited in Case 16, in which readers consider how the CEO of a long-term care facility tried to deal with long-term staffing issues, despite a limited budget. The questions and readings below build on these themes of employee retention and motivation.

Part V Cases

Case 14, "Employee Retention in a PR Firm: Generational Differences or Insufficient Incentives?," examines the challenges faced by Cindy Yueh, owner of *Join Public Relations* (JPR), a public relations agency that specialized in promoting luxury brands in Taiwan. She recently turned down lucrative contracts due to insufficient staff and wanted to know what she could do to retain young employees. Yueh preferred to hire young people, because she believed that they were more technology savvy, but was starting to believe that generational differences were in play when it came to recruitment and retention. It became increasingly difficult for her to find qualified entry level applicants and even harder to keep them for more than a couple of years. The majority of non-managers worked at JPR for under 1 year. Yueh tried several unsuccessful and unconventional approaches and perks to increase retention.

The learning objectives for this case include:

- Students will analyze and identify issues associated with employee retention.
- Students will apply motivation theories and relate them to employee engagement.

Case 15, "Colleagues or Sloths? Collaboration and the Allocation of Credit for Contribution," gives multiple examples of colleagues not following through on promises. It features Gloria Wainwright who had agreed to be the project manager of an initiative

DOI: 10.4324/9781003326298-21

to publish a collection of business cases. Collectively it was intended to meet accreditation requirements, and individually the authors would comply with expectations that they were conducting research. Gloria recruited coworkers who agreed to research and write business cases and to also provide detailed reviews of each other's manuscripts. That collaborative approach was to ensure their efforts resulted in high quality teaching cases. As months went by, she noted few cases were finished, and reviews were delayed or never completed.

The learning objectives for this case include:

- Students analyze and identify issues associated around expectation setting in work groups.
- Students practice discussing unmet expectations in collaborative work.

Case 16, "Sandy Shores Care Center: A Long-Term Care Staffing Crisis," examines the human resources challenges faced by Sarah Martin, CEO of Sandy Shores Care Center. Like any long-term care facility in the US, the center struggled with optimal staffing levels to provide excellent care to residents in the building. Sarah and her leadership team had to conduct an analysis of their current staffing retention practices, consider new ideas for implementation, and be mindful of a limited budget available. Sarah needed to present a report to SSCC's Board of Directors with a plan to improve their staffing issues.

The learning objectives for this case include:

- Consider and evaluate current organizational staffing retention tactics in a long-term care facility.
- Research and recommend an impactful cost-effective approach to retention.

Part V Supplemental Questions

Reflection Questions

1. What are the characteristics of an engaged employee in your workplace? How are they differentiated from employees who are considered disengaged?
2. When it comes to employee engagement, to what extent do you believe it is the responsibility of the manager to foster employee engagement versus the responsibility of the employees themselves to remain engaged?
3. What motivates you to do your best work? To what extent are your motivators internally generated versus from external sources? Is there a situation where those motivators might not be as effective for you?

Discussion Questions

1. What do the three cases have in common regarding how the managers or team leaders approached others' motivation?
2. What recommendations would you offer to the managers in these cases regarding the best approaches to address the current retention or motivation problems with their employees?

3.   How might the situations of employee turnover or disengagement in the three cases have been prevented?

Part V Related Readings

Employee Retention

Carucci, R. (2021). To retain employees, give them a sense of purpose and community. *Harvard Business Review*, October 11. Accessed at https://hbr.org/2021/10/to-retain-employees-give-them-a-sense-of-purpose-and-community

Crail, C. & Watts, R. (2023). 15 effective employee retention strategies in 2024. Accessed at www.forbes.com/advisor/business/employee-retention-strategies/

Robert Half. (2023). 14 effective employee retention strategies. Accessed at www.roberthalf.com/us/en/insights/management-tips/effective-employee-retention-strategies

Employee Motivation

Dowd, M. (2021). How to deal with coworkers who don't do their part in the project. *Houston Chronicle*, June 21. Accessed at https://work.chron.com/deal-coworkers-dont-part-project-2431.html

Kaado, B. (2023). Money isn't enough: 6 Incentives to motivate your employees. *Business News Daily*, October 20. Accessed at www.businessnewsdaily.com/10731-money-not-enough.html

Knight, R. (2021). When you're stuck working with a slacker. *Harvard Business Review*, May 14. Accessed at https://hbr.org/2021/05/when-youre-stuck-working-with-a-slacker

Case 14   Employee Retention in a PR Firm
Generational Differences or Insufficient Incentives?

Holly Chiu and Laurie L. Levesque

Synopsis

Cindy Yueh owned Join Public Relations (JPR), a public relations agency that specialized in promoting luxury brands in Taiwan. She turned down lucrative contracts due to insufficient staff and wanted to know what she could do to retain young employees. Yueh preferred to hire young people, because she believed that they were more technology savvy. It was increasingly difficult to find qualified entry level applicants and even harder to keep them for more than a couple of years. The majority of non-managers worked there for under one year. Yueh tried several unconventional approaches and perks to increase retention.

Turning away Potential Clients

Cindy Yueh finished her call with a regional manager of the luxury brand Tory Burch. It was February, 2023 and the second time they contacted her company, Join Public Relations (JPR). Previously, in December, a manager at Tory Burch approached JPR requesting an annual contract to cover all events for the year 2023. Yueh regretfully told them that her company did not have the capacity to take on their job. Tory Burch then shopped around, but JPR was repeatedly recommended to them. Yueh turned them down a second time; she still had insufficient staff to take on that project. Unfortunately, JPR's inability to provide services to Tory Burch was not an exception. Yueh felt the constant pressure of recruiting, as a shortage of employees resulted in these lost opportunities. She started to think that she couldn't fix the recruiting problem, and wondered if she changed the way she managed whether her employees would stay longer.

Company Background

Cindy Yueh started JPR in 2004, a public relations (PR) agency specializing in event planning, media management, and the marketing of luxury brands in Taiwan. JPR worked with world-famous brands, such as Tiffany, Bulgari, Hermes, and Louis Vuitton on new product launch parties, press conferences, and other events that promoted each brand's image. Even though JPR was the leading agency for luxury brands in Taiwan, Yueh wanted to differentiate herself from her competitors even more by providing the general public with behind-the-scenes insights into the creative industry. In 2017, she

DOI: 10.4324/9781003326298-22

created a new digital media platform at JPR called "Wazaiii" and hired editors to write articles, shoot short films, and conduct interviews with experts in the creative industry, such as show directors, brand managers, and make-up artists. More than 70 writers produced online columns each month. In addition, she held paid, one-day, in-person workshops for people interested in working in the creative or the PR industries. In 2020, due to the pandemic, those were offered online, which later became another business line. JPR called it "Wazaiii online" and offered a variety of virtual classes, workshops, and webinars, ranging from fashion to workplace mentoring. JPR thus provided online-offline integrated services to clients, and became a bridge for the general public to have deeper knowledge of those brands as well as the whole industry.

Yueh recognized that many young people were initially attracted to the PR industry due to the glamour, i.e., they had the opportunity to work with stars and celebrities. However, the industry was also notorious for long working hours with lower-than-average salaries for entry-level positions. For example, the salary survey at 104 Job Bank (2024), a leading online job search website in Taiwan, showed that the average salary for those with less than one year of working experience in the financial industry was 21% higher than those in the PR industry, and engineering-related jobs were at least 30.4% higher than the PR industry. The PR industry as a whole had problems with employee retention, especially with younger staff. On average, the turnover rate for employees with less than two years was 70%. Entry-level PR employees only received a big jump in salary after 5–6 years of working in the industry and JPR's staffing pattern was no exception. It had 28 staff members and eight managers. Most managers had been there since Yueh first started the company; even the most junior manager had worked there for 10 years. However, there were only nine staff members who had worked at JPR for over two years, which meant nearly 20 employees had a tenure shorter than one year.

In recent years, a number of JPR's younger employees had resigned to pursue advanced degrees. However, Yueh witnessed that sometimes those previous employees returned to the same industry after two years of study. She recalled a conversation a few years ago with one of her best employees, Sharon Lin. Lin worked at JPR for 2.5 years as an Account Executive; it was her first job. She was smart and efficient, and also calm and organized, which was helpful in the fast-paced world of public relations. Yueh believed that Lin had great potential to be successful in the industry, and considered promoting her to manager. However, Lin told Yueh that she planned to resign to pursue an advanced degree. Yueh suggested she should postpone that plan for two years, because if she wanted to return later, that additional industry experience would make a huge difference. "After 2 years of studying, if you come back to the same industry, you still have 2.5 years of experience, but you will be competing with someone like you with 5 years of experience." Yueh then asked if Lin wanted a transfer to another team along with a pay raise, but Lin declined everything Yueh proposed.

Yueh also discovered that many previous employees did not actually pursue an advanced degree after leaving as they claimed. Some went to other PR companies, some changed industries, and some did nothing. She always gave her best wishes to employees who parted with JPR, but she did not understand why some of them just stayed home and did nothing. "It is okay if they changed to other jobs, but I don't understand why some people just did nothing. They didn't study, they didn't find another job. I feel like I don't understand their logic and I don't understand what they value."

Yueh's Management Style

Yueh's passion for media and public relations was ignited with her first job as a fundraising officer for a non-profit organization. She fell in love with the liveliness and excitement that type of job brought almost immediately. She also knew it would be impossible to enter the PR industry without related working experience and a network of contacts. To this end, she worked for a movie company and connected with PR agencies because of her responsibilities for the marketing activities of an award-winning film. She later accepted a job at a PR agency where she worked extremely hard and was very disciplined. Although the company was flexible about attendance, Yueh mimicked her manager and was in her office no later than 9:30 a.m. Even after she became a manager herself, she was in the office no later than 10:00 a.m. no matter how late she worked the night before. It was not that she wanted to be different from others, but simply because she felt there was too much work to finish. Her motto was "Exceed others' expectations."

Yueh started JPR when she turned 30 and brought that same discipline to her own company. She called herself the "Miranda Priestly in the PR industry" or the "Devil boss," referring to the main character of the movie *The Devil Wears Prada*. She observed what leading companies did and implemented some of the same. She also implemented policies which none of the other PR agencies in Taiwan had. "Since I am the boss, I can do things I believe are right in my company, regardless of what anyone else is doing," Yueh said. She had never taken management courses, and had learned to manage by doing. The first thing she introduced was an attendance rule: all employees had to be in the office by 9:30 a.m. with 15 minutes flexibility. If they could not make it in on time, they had to take personal leave. Other PR agencies in Taiwan allowed employees to start their workday at any time they preferred, mostly because they usually worked long hours and finished their work quite late, sometimes even past midnight. Whenever employees challenged her about the policy, Yueh commented:

> It was not uncommon if you called any PR agencies in Taiwan and no one answered the phone in the morning because most people would not show up in the office until after lunch. I do not like that. If we all had to work in the office late the night before, why would it be fair that someone came to the office at 9ish in the morning while others came after lunch but got the same pay? In addition, all work was teamwork. If someone was slow or not disciplined, the whole team had to stop or to do extra to cover that person, which makes the working hours even longer.

Yueh provided overtime pay, which was also something unheard of in the industry. It was normal in PR agencies for employees to work more than 10 hours a day. Paying overtime was avoided because it was assumed that it would have cost business owners a fortune. However, Yueh believed it was a good motivator for her employees:

> Working long hours is a norm in this industry. For example, when we had an event, we might have to be there at 9:00 a.m. but could not leave the site until one or two the next morning. Not to mention the weeks before the event, we all worked 'til midnight. Also, the salary of the entry-level employees was relatively low. Consequently, I had employees filing for resignation because they wanted a job with shorter hours and higher salary.

Interestingly, she found out employees reacted differently with regard to the overtime pay. Those holding administrative roles, such as human resource officer or book-keeper, tended to apply for the overtime pay more often. For example, if they were late for work by a half an hour, they would stay half an hour later on the same day and applied for the overtime pay for that half an hour. On the other hand, many event planners and website editors kept working even after they got home, but would always forget to apply for the overtime pay. She constantly had to remind them to apply for the overtime pay.

Employee Retention at JPR

Yueh was 50 years old and hired younger people whom she believed to be more energetic and technology-savvy, especially for Wazaiii. Her non-manager employees ranged in age from 23 to 31 years old. She tried many things that she thought should have appealed to younger people. For example, she hired college students as interns, and posted JPR's job openings on Wazaiii. Applicants took a written test to show their PR knowledge; those who had previous experience also wrote a proposal. JPR paid salaries higher than the market rate. Their job title "Account Executive" was changed to "Integrated Marketing Executive" because Yueh heard the younger generation pre-ferred marketing-related jobs. She also believed they had different work values, such as wanting to be "seen." Therefore, each year she handpicked a few employees and worked with them directly on a big project or assigned them to work on the year-end staff party, which was equivalent to a big PR party, but focused internally. She held an annual team-building retreat and the company paid for international travel for all employees once a year.

However, she noticed that younger employees wanted to have an easier life with acceptable salary. The PR industry required very long working hours and workers had to sacrifice their time with their family and friends:

> In PR, you have to love challenges, be flexible, and be patient. You need to communicate with clients and wait for them to respond and then integrate what they want into what you are working on, even at the last minute. It is not a dull job, rather, it is *too* interesting: many things happening at the same time and many details to take care of.

Despite this, she had few job applicants and ongoing problems with a high turnover rate. She wanted to know what else she could do to attract and retain younger employees; it was not good for JPR to turn away clients due to staffing issues.

Reflection Questions

1.   Can you think of a time when an employer or manager tried to motivate you to perform your job or tasks differently, but their approach was mismatched with what truly motivates you? What was the situation?
2.   Think about a time you quit a job, volunteer position, team, or professional association. To what extent did the leader(s) attempt to understand and do something about why people like you left the organization? To what extent were you fully truthful explaining your reasons for leaving?

Learning Applications

1. Analyze this situation using two course concepts, frameworks, or model.
2. Interview a manager to learn why people leave their company. How is employee turnover handled, i.e., does the company actively try to minimize it or is it accepted as a normal aspect of business operations?

Reference

104 Job Bank. (2024). Salary. Accessed at: https://guide.104.com.tw/salary.

Related Readings

Babel Work Blog. (2019). Top five marks of great PR company culture. Accessed at: https://babelpr.com/top-five-marks-of-great-pr-company-culture/.

Indeed Editorial Team. (2023). 16 reasons why employees choose to leave their jobs. Accessed at: www.indeed.com/career-advice/career-development/reasons-employees-leave.

Pruit, J. (2016). What motivates your employees? 5 ways to figure it out. Accessed at: www.inc.com/jeff-pruitt/5-ways-to-find-out-what-drives-your-employees.html.

Case 15   Colleagues or Sloths?

Collaboration and the Allocation of Credit for Contribution

Gina Vega

Synopsis

Gloria Wainwright had mentored peers who dealt with team members who over-promised or underdelivered in research projects. She expected a different outcome when she agreed to be the project manager of her college's initiative to publish a collection of business cases. The coworkers she recruited had all agreed to research and write business cases and to also provide detailed reviews of each other's manuscripts. That collaborative approach was to ensure that output would result in high quality teaching cases. As the months went by, she noted fewer cases were finished than promised, and reviews were delayed or not completed.

Colleagues or Sloths?

> The sloth is the world's slowest mammal, so sedentary that algae grow on its furry coat ... Sloths are identified by the number of long, prominent claws that they have on each front foot. There are both two-toed and three-toed sloths. All sloths are built for life in the treetops. They spend nearly all of their time aloft, hanging from branches with a powerful grip aided by their long claws. (Dead sloths have been known to retain their grip and remain suspended from a branch.) Sloths even sleep in trees, and they sleep a lot – some 15 to 20 hours every day. Even when awake they often remain motionless.
>
> (*National Geographic*)[1]

"Hmmm," murmured Gloria[2] as she read this description. "I actually have a few colleagues who fit this description exactly, including some with whom I have collaborated. It's just like when my students complain that it isn't fair when they do all the work, yet a slacking teammate gets full credit. It seems like free-riding behavior happens in all work environments."

Generosity or Taking Advantage?

Gloria Wainwright was an active academic, prolific scholar, and a frequent collaborator in publishing research papers. She had a long history of mentoring colleagues, students, and even strangers who requested help in her areas of expertise. Her philosophy of collaboration on manuscripts was simple: Anyone can manage to work with someone else for the duration of one project. You never have to collaborate on a

DOI: 10.4324/9781003326298-23

second project if you don't like the other person's work process or believe there is a mismatch of knowledge or skills. She also believed strongly in Harry Truman's famous words: "It's amazing what you can accomplish if you don't care who gets the credit." This philosophy sometimes led Gloria into trouble.

Gloria reflected on a time when she acted as a consultant for a colleague who was working on a business case with two other academics. Their case was about operational issues in a hotel, and the three co-authors spent considerable time on site observing and interviewing hotel employees. Gloria thought everything would be fine as the research team seemed motivated to get the case written quickly and efficiently and they had divided up the writing of some of the sections. The problems only arose when the lead author received drafts from the other writers. They were poorly written, ill-conceived in focus and content, and did not even follow any of the stylistic conventions of case writing. The lead author held a meeting of the three where she explained again the case writing protocols. She then asked the two coauthors to make specific changes and resend their sections to her.

The other two authors smiled agreeably and promised to deliver. The following week, when she inquired, they promised again. And the next week, it happened again. This went on for nearly the entire semester, with the lead author reporting again and again to Gloria about her collaborators' noncompliance. Finally, the lead author could stand it no longer and just wrote the entire case herself. Needless to say, the other two authors expected their names to appear on the case as contributing co-authors. Ultimately, they did.

After thinking about this situation for a while, Gloria realized it was not an isolated incident. She thought about a few times when she had been in the same situation. The feeling of frustration appeared with force after she wrote a paper with one of her colleagues and that person's frequent writing partner. The third person never actually participated in the writing of their manuscript; nonetheless, Gloria's colleagues insisted that person's name be included. In the interests of getting the paper written and published, Gloria agreed to include the third person's name. But Gloria refused to do it a second time. She drew the line when her colleague wanted the friend's name included on a case on which that person had had no input. Her colleague argued, "But you can put *your* name on *our* other manuscript." Gloria rejected that proposal, saying "No, I do not want my name on your paper, because I had nothing to do with that project ... I contributed nothing and it is not my work." Gloria held firm and the third author's name did not appear on the second manuscript.

Retired in Place

"Nobody likes to be taken advantage of," Gloria thought. "Not even by friends. Especially when those friends act like they are 'Retired in Place' (RIP)." The tenure system in the university encouraged an RIP-perspective for some tenured faculty who perceived that the pressure to keep publishing no longer applied to them. Some faculty members simply stopped researching or publishing and focused solely on teaching their classes. However, there was a lot of work behind the scenes to keep the school running, and faculty had an important service contribution on committees that dealt with policy, curriculum development, and administrative work related to the academic departments. Additionally, accreditors and administrators expected timely research publications to signal that faculty were current with business trends. So, having colleagues with an RIP mindset meant that the onus of school's service work and scholarly publication fell to others in the department to accomplish. This, in turn, put too much work at the feet of those faculty who continued to produce.

Gloria faced just such a situation. She was compiling a collection of published cases for use in her school, and each case was to be written by her coworkers. In addition, her colleagues had agreed to peer review any new cases written and submitted for inclusion in the collection These submissions couldn't be blind reviewed, i. e., reviewers could guess which of their colleagues had written the cases. However, they could still be peer-reviewed and held to a high standard to ensure the published works represented the school well. More than half the faculty had promised to make themselves available to review and help their less experienced peers write, revise, and publish their work in a timely fashion.

As the deadlines approached, faculty members contributed less. Suddenly they were no longer available to review peers' cases, or they did not have time to write the cases to which they had committed. Somehow, the press of daily teaching overwhelmed them, despite having decades of experience with that courseload.

Gloria was left with a shortage of cases for the promised collection, a shortage of case reviewers to mentor the cases to completion, and an abundance of work she had to cover for others. She couldn't help but wonder if this was the lazy kind of sloth or the two-faced kind, where commitments were ignored and self-interest prevailed.

Reflection Questions

1. Have you ever had teammates who promised to complete their share of the work and then did not? How did the team handle the situation? What could you have done that might have led to a different outcome?
2. Have you ever been in a project group and agreed to take responsibility for a task but then were unable to meet the deadline? What prevented you from finishing the work on time? What could the team leader or your peers have done differently? What could you have done differently?

Learning Applications

1. Research best practices around setting expectations when working with peers. What five practices might you use as a team member? What practices should your manager use to reduce instances of people getting credit for work they did not complete.
2. Interview a manager about issues and expectations setting related to subordinates' work contribution, deadlines, and collaboration. What are the greatest challenges? What facilitates it?

Related Readings

Forbes Coaches Council. (2023). How to hold employees accountable when they don't follow through. Accessed at: www.forbes.com/sites/forbescoachescouncil/2023/03/21/how-to-hold-employees-accountable-when-they-dont-follow-through/

O'Hara, C. (2017). How to work with someone who isn't a team player. Accessed at: https://hbr.org/2017/04/how-to-work-with-someone-who-isnt-a-team-player

Rampton, J. (2021). What should you do when team members aren't pulling their weight? Accessed at: www.entrepreneur.com/leadership/what-should-you-do-when-team-members-arent-pulling-their/362195

Notes

1 See http://animals.nationalgeographic.com/animals/mammals/three-toed-sloth/
2 All names, organizations, and locations are anonymized.

Case 16 Sandy Shores Care Center

A Long-Term Care Staffing Crisis

Lindsey J. G. Creapeau and Kevin Hansen

Synopsis

Sarah Martin, CEO of Sandy Shores Care Center, was faced with a significant direct care staffing challenge in her skilled nursing center. She and her leadership team had to conduct an analysis of their current staffing retention practices, consider new ideas for implementation, and be mindful of a limited budget available. Sarah needed to present a report to SSCC's Board of Directors with a plan to improve their staffing issues.

Sandy Shores Care Center

Sarah Martin, CEO of Sandy Shores Care Center, Minnesota, USA, was attending her daily leadership stand-up meeting held in May of 2014. Stand-up meeting attendees generally included her direct reports Megan VanEckel, the nursing home administrator (NHA) and Sue Sherman, director of human resources; as well as Tammy Ohm, director of nursing (DON) and other department heads. The group met each weekday at 9:00 a.m. to discuss census, changes in resident condition, and any other pertinent organizational business. The DON, Tammy, started the stand up by sharing her concern regarding staffing. She emphasized her position by stating, "This is not sustainable. We're at our breaking point. We need more staff. I need help." Sarah and the rest of the team heard Tammy loud and clear, exchanging concerned glances.

Sarah Martin

Having previously worked as an NHA, Sarah was hired as the CEO of Sandy Shores Care Center in the fall of 2010 (see Figure 16.1). Sandy Shores was a continuing care retirement community (CCRC), with a skilled nursing facility, assisted living, memory care, adult day care, hospice, and home health care provided to the residents and members of the surrounding neighborhood. Over the past 10 years, Sarah had emerged as a dynamic, intelligent, and engaged leader in the post-acute care field in the state of Minnesota. As a lifelong learner, she continued to pursue her education and in 2012 earned her Juris Doctor and active law license. Sarah was well-known in the post-acute care field for being both an advocate for her industry and a successful leader. Under Sarah's leadership, Sandy Shores' expansion of service lines, increases in profitability, and low staff turnover rates were frequently highlighted by state provider associations.

DOI: 10.4324/9781003326298-24

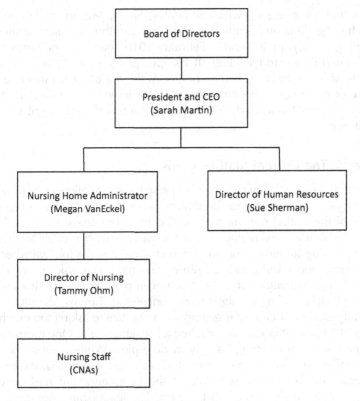

Figure 16.1 Sandy Shores organizational chart (partial).

Past Success in Addressing Staffing Issues

Staffing crises, and the ability to quickly rebound, were nothing new to Sarah. During her first week on the job in 2010, she attended the organization's Board of Directors meeting. Dennis Chastain, the Board Chairman, was direct with her. He said:

> Sarah, the nursing home here at Sandy Shores Care Center has a big staffing pro-blem. As CEO, we need you to work with both the NHA and your Human Resources Director to fill the open direct care staff positions we have. It's a lot. We have 19 open positions and we're using agency staff for about six shifts per week. I know I don't need to tell you this, but agency costs almost double what it would take for us to have our own staff members working those positions. We're hoping you can eliminate the use of this agency staff within 30 days. We're doing okay in our other service lines, but we really need to turn around our numbers in the skilled nursing facility. The deficit is too big to maintain and keep us viable.

Sarah took the request to heart. She made this initiative her top priority in her first month on the job. She quickly teamed up with her NHA Megan and her HR director Sue to determine what recruitment and retention efforts were in place and what could be added, enhanced, or discontinued. This was an all-hands-on-deck effort for the three leaders, who knew they were under a tight timeline. After tirelessly recruiting, interviewing, and following up with candidates, Sarah, Megan, and Sue concluded the 30 days having eliminated staffing agency use, and thus terminating their contract with the staffing agency. By the end of February 2010, the numbers were clear: Sandy Shores had turned it around by filling all 19 open positions and had been able to fill all open shifts with the staff they had on board. At the March board meeting, Sarah felt a huge sense of pride when the financials were reviewed and staffing costs were no longer above budget. Dennis said, "On behalf of the board, way to go! We knew you were a great hire."

Flash Forward: The Current Staffing Crisis

Over the next four years, staffing continued to present some challenges as usual. As CEO, Sarah was not actively involved in the day-to-day operations of the human resources activities nor of the skilled nursing facility. She had confidence in Sue's 16 years of experience in recruitment and retention, and Sue had always been able to "figure it out." As the nursing home administrator, Megan had done a great job with her staff, too. Between overtime hours and continual hiring, Sue had been able to keep the use of agency staff at bay. In January of 2014, Sue began periodically mentioning that their skilled nursing facility staffing numbers were concerning. Tammy, the DON, reiterated this periodically, stating, "Our staff is getting worn out. We're asking too much of them."

By May of 2014, the situation had reached a breaking point. One morning, during a leadership team standup meeting, Tammy made a plea. While great at their jobs, her direct care staff were overworked, overwhelmed, and exhausted. There were too many vacancies in the staffing schedule at the time, and staff had become more unwilling to work extra shifts to cover the gaps. The leadership team knew that there was generally a high morale and low turnover rate (for the long-term care industry) at Sandy Shores, but after Tammy's statement, Sarah asked the rest of the group what they had heard from workers, specifically about staffing. Overwhelmingly, leaders said that their reports shared feelings of concern, agitation, upset, and frustration. Other than the open positions, this was one of Sarah's biggest areas of concern. The leadership team had told her that staff were complaining that "the leadership team wasn't doing anything" to solve the staffing problems. Sue replied, "I just don't know what else to do. Maybe we need to rethink how we've approached this."

While human resources and staffing were not her direct area of responsibility, Sarah was ultimately accountable for maintaining a fiscally sound budget and had a personal sense of responsibility to help based on the communication from her board years earlier. As a previous NHA, Sarah believed that if you took great care of staff, they would take care of residents; in short, high staff satisfaction reflected an excellent care center. Additionally, Sarah had previously worked as a certified nursing assistant (CNA) and kept her license up to date. Her prior knowledge of the day-to-day struggles working short-staffed motivated her to find a solution for her care center. Sarah suggested that she, Megan, and Sue, who had successfully tackled the issue in 2010, reconvene to revisit their plan. They put a meeting date on their calendar for the following week.

Quantifying the Staffing Problem

Once together, Sue shared the numbers with Sarah and Megan. At that time, there were a total of 106 direct-care CNA staff employed at SSCC, with 14 direct-care CNA positions open in the skilled nursing facility. Some of these were full-time positions, but others were part-time. Her vacancies totaled 7.7 full-time employees (FTEs).

As CEO, Sarah could be as creative as she wanted to be in staffing, but she had to be mindful of her budget as Sandy Shores was a nonprofit organization. She had $10,633 budgeted each month for staffing recruitment and retention initiatives. Ultimately, upon recommendations from local partners, the three decided to hire an agency to offload recruitment efforts. SSCC hired "as needed" (i.e., PRN) recruitment service for $8,400 per month rather than resorting to the prior practice of using agency staff to fill open shifts, which was exponentially more expensive. With that task covered, SSCC was left with the issue of retaining the current staff they had, and the group could be flexible with the remaining $2,233 per month.

Sue shared her thoughts on the staffing issues they were experiencing. One of her concerns was competition. The past few years had brought increased competition in the local labor market from other care homes and service-related businesses including retail, restaurants, and hotels, as more businesses were established and/or moved to the area. Sandy Shores offered competitive wages at the 75th percentile in CNA wages for all positions at the care center based on statewide association data for peer organizations (medium-sized, freestanding, nonprofit, West Central region). However, Sue had data showing that their wages were occasionally lower than those in other industries, e.g., production workers, delivery drivers, furniture sales professionals.

Sue indicated that staff turnover for CNAs was not optimal at 49.8%, but it was lower than the state and national averages (51.1% and 51.6%, respectively) as was the rate for RN turnover. This retention had allowed for residents to work with familiar caregivers, given that Sandy Shores utilized consistent staff assignment practices, which provided comfort to residents and their family members.

Human Resources regularly conducted stay interviews with staff. Stay interviews asked staff members about aspects of their jobs that were working well and what Sandy Shores could do to continue to foster a welcoming work environment. These interviews were conducted at 30, 60, and 90 days post-hire and during annual performance evaluations. Stay interviews consistently echoed findings from the past employee satisfaction surveys, yet official metrics were not collected or regularly reviewed. Direct care staff valued their supervisor Tammy, saw her as a strong and effective leader, and appreciated her for encouraging and modeling a welcoming work environment. Staff were hard-working, engaged, and passionate.

Staff members that were past their probationary period generally reported high morale. In fact, past internal employee satisfaction surveys indicated that 100% of staff would recommend Sandy Shores as a great place to work to friends and family (although a survey had not been conducted recently). However, Tammy approached Sue earlier in the month to let her know that at least one CNA quit after three weeks on the job because of how she was treated. As was the case in other care centers, seasoned CNAs historically seemed to be tough on new employees. Sarah, Sue, and Megan shared feelings of frustration about this; they didn't understand how those staff members couldn't see the "big picture." Sarah felt that a new team member meant less work was on the horizon for the team as a whole, if they could just make it through training.

Sue reminded Sarah and Megan that the organization's retention committee had been meeting biweekly, and the group advised leadership of novel suggestions or concerns related to retention techniques that were working, could work, or were not working. They had implemented potluck meals, a gratitude board for staff, holiday parties, and themed weekly activities, but the same staff had been part of this committee for quite a few years.

Sandy Shores had not used agency staff in recent years, but rather had a large internal float pool of current staff to cover open shifts. This was beneficial in that employees often wanted to pick up shifts, residents had caregivers with whom they were familiar, and staff were paid at a higher rate for taking on unpopular shifts ($1 per hour more for overnight, or 1.5 times pay for weekends). However, staff were burning out and overtime costs were climbing, resulting in staff members who were less willing to pick up extra shifts. Sarah recalled previous discussions of reconsidering their current staffing pattern of 8-hour shifts with a 30-minute unpaid lunch break (which was consistent with local long-term care competitors). The team also discussed reviewing fringe-benefits offered to CNAs outlined in the job description (paid holidays and vacation; short term disability; dental, health, vision, and life insurance; 403(b) retirement savings plan; free on-site fitness center; benefits could be waived for additional pay) to see if there were low- or no-cost strategies that could further enhance employee satisfaction. To this point, however, they had not revisited the idea of exploring more flexible shift options or other benefits that were offered by competitors, such as discounted partnerships with childcare or restaurants, free on-site health screenings, or use of the fitness center.

Action Needed

As CEO, Sarah could be as creative as she wanted to be in staffing, but she had to be mindful of her budget as Sandy Shores was a nonprofit organization. With staff recruitment being addressed, she and the team needed to decide the best course of action to retain their current staff despite the barriers presented. From her years of experience, Sarah determined that what the team needed to do was to develop a plan related to their current staffing issues. They needed to keep the CMS 5-star rating of SSCC in mind compared to local competitors before working to craft a sustainable solution for the problem. Sarah needed to present a plan to outline how to increase retention of CNA staff at the next board meeting in four weeks' time.

Reflection Questions

1. Consider an organization where you currently (or previously) work or volunteer. Are its efforts to retain staff similar or different from what is done at Sandy Shores? Why might that be the case?
2. What leadership practices might have contributed to or hindered the retention of employees at Sandy Shores? What alternatives are there?

Learning Applications

1. Analyze the situation at Sandy Shores using two course concepts, frameworks, or models so as to offer insights into what happened.
2. Research creative and effective practices for retaining staff at senior care, assisted living, or nursing home facilities. What recommendations would be useful at Sandy Shores?

Related Readings

De Vries, N., Boone, A., Godderis, L., Bouman, J., Szemik, S., Matranga, D., & de Winter, P. (2023). The race to retain healthcare workers: A systematic review on factors that impact retention of nurses and physicians in hospitals. *Inquiry: A Journal of Medical Care Organization, Provision and Financing*, 60. Accessed at: www.ncbi.nlm.nih.gov/pmc/articles/PMC10014988/

Kempton, B. (2022). The best alternative staffing solutions for 2023. Accessed at: www.upwork.com/resources/guide-alternative-staffing-solutions

Acknowledgement

The full version of this case was originally published by the authors in the *International Journal of Instructional Cases* (2022). It has been adapted for this volume with permission of the publisher and author.

Index

Printed in the United States
by Baker & Taylor Publisher Services